Goodnight Children, Everywhere

Dedication

To my five daughters:

Marguerita, Angela, Francesca, Lucia, Georgina

To my ten grandchildren:

Selina, Elizabeth, Adam, Victoria, Julia, Felicity, Courtney, Grant, Eloise and Richard Paul.

For the smile they put on my face every time they raise their eyes to heaven - when I mention the war.

Goodnight Children, Everywhere

(Uncle Mac: BBC Children's Hour 1939 - 1945)

by

Rose McNamara-Wright

SOUTH OXHEY PUBLISHING

ISBN 0-9533569-0-6

Typeset by Amolibros, Watchet, Somerset
Publication of this title has been managed by Amolibros
Printed and bound by Professional Book Supplies, Oxford,
England

Contents

Acknowledgements

I would like to thank the many people who have helped me in various ways, making this book possible: Wendy Burns, Vanessa Levy, Anette Nugent, my tutors in English; Ester Klein, my patient IT tutor; John and Kay Horsfield and Jennifer Yates-Rowe, my best friends and proof readers; Bill Endell for his part as proof reader; Mike Banks for his kind permission to let me use extracts from his Borneo article in the *Saga Magazine;* Terry Hassey and Racheal Brown just for being there to egg me on when I flagged; John Arthur Bailey, my cousin, for supplying his reminiscences in Chapter Seven; all my friends at Cassio College and all the Senior Citizens who have told me things and put me right about a date or two.

I hope I have not upset anyone in my story. If I have, it was unintentional. If I have left anything out that is important to you, I am very sorry. But if I had written down all that I had wanted this book would have been too big and heavy to lift. Thanks to all of you.

V . . . ▬

Preface

Fifty-five million people were killed in the Second World War: military personnel and civilians; mothers, fathers, children, whole families, friends and pets. The death toll in this war was higher than any other war in recorded history. This war was fought to destroy tyranny, which it has done for us for the last fifty-odd years. But wars still go on all over the world; in this world there are enough weapons to destroy all life on earth. Countless millions yearn for a world without conflict and war. Most of us are searching for peace and security - our own Garden of Eden, our own Utopia, our city of gold, a place where no fears or terrors lurk for us. Yet, while trying to make these things come true, it is our own aspirations which result in wars, revolution, pain and suffering. Our twentieth century has been the least peaceful century in history. The Queen Mother said in her speech to the women of Britain in 1945, "Maybe what we women have suffered in this war may indirectly save our children and our grandchildren from another." Let us hope so.

V . . . —

About this book

This book has been written for anyone who lived through the last war (World War II), and for anyone who was a child during that war and suffered as only children can. It is for the brave mothers who had to face bombs falling on them and their children, night after night and day after day - all alone and without their menfolk. It is for the women - women who, against all odds, steeled their nerves and got up and got out to work, either in the munitions factories, the Auxiliary Fire Services, Ambulance and First Aid Post, (even as drivers); Light Rescue and Civil Defence. Others helped by looking after the children and running canteens and generally keeping our bodies and soul together. Everyone played their part, even the children. Children played a big part in this most awful war and suffered in many, many ways, without complaint.

Most of the information in this book is written from the memory of a little London girl who was a six-year-old when World War II started and a twelve-year-old when it ended. It is about what happened before the war, during the war, what happened at the end of the war and the consequences of that terrible war. Some accounts, because the memory plays tricks, may wander a little from the actual time and date but they are all authentic. Some dates I could not possibly have known I have learnt from other people (see bibliography). I hope you enjoy my book and that it brings back some of your own memories.

V . . . ━

VEE, DOT. DOT. DOT. DASH - the V for Victory Campaign

'I know we are told we should not to live in the past, and I agree, but we should not lose sight of the past. The human memory is not very reliable, and with the passing of time memories can become dim or over-exaggerated. We all remember things differently, some one way, others another way. They are our memories.' Quoted from the book by the same author, *South Oxhey: A Giant On Their Doorstep* by Rose McNamara-Wright

V . . . ___ V . . . ___ V . . . ___

V . . . ___ V . . . ___ V . . . ___

Morse coded message in 1945 - Victory in Europe.
Vee. dot. dot. dot. Dash - the V for Victory Campaign.

V . . . ___

Prologue

I was born in 1933 in the middle of the depression. Most people at that time were very poor and there was no work for them to do. Some families were starving and their children were dying of hunger.

Why anyone would want to bring children into the world at that time beats me, but good job Dad got a twinkle in his eye, or I would never have got here.

I was six when the Second World War started, and living in Finsbury Park, where we had moved to from Islington after my birth. We had to move many times during the war and for various reasons - mostly because of the bomb blasts and the damage they did which made our homes unsafe. But that was not always the case. Sometimes we had to dodge the rent man.

We lived through the war and we are living through the peace; none of it has been easy. But we have picked ourselves up, we have dusted ourselves off and we have started again.

I married in 1955 and brought five beautiful daughters into this world, who in their turn married five handsome fellows and gave me ten beautiful grandchildren. We all live near each other. For me life is beautiful now.

V . . . ___

Introduction

Non bastardo carborundum

(Don't let the bastards grind you down)

This has been my motto for the best part of my life. It has stood me in good stead as I have faced the ups and downs of living with the consequences of my own deeds and the deeds of others that have affected me.

The first part of my life was relatively carefree. Children in those days were treated like children and grown-ups never spoke about grown-up things in front of them; they would just say, "Shssh, not in front of the children." I must admit that made our ears prick up. My brother Bill and I always tried to listen to our parents talking to each other but it all seemed rather dull and boring and we didn't understand most of what they said. It was always about war and someone Dad called a "bloody war-monger". I found out much later that it was Winston Churchill he was referring to. You may have gathered by that my dad didn't like him. The conversation was much more interesting when my Mum and her sisters got together.

V. . . ▬

Things took an abrupt change on Sunday the 3rd of September 1939; war broke out. What did it mean? Nothing different had happened as far as we children could tell, although somehow we knew something *was* different. We knew it was serious this time, we could tell by the look on the faces of our mum and dad and it frightened us. War and preparation for war was not new to us. It had been the only topic of conversation we children had ever heard for most of our young lives. It seemed to us kids that the war had started with a speech from the Prime Minister, Mr Chamberlain who just said, "This country is now at war with Germany; we are ready."

We had been listening to the wireless as usual. Everyone did in those days (it was never off) and we had heard what the Prime Minister had said: this country was now at war with Germany. There seemed to be a stunned silence, then lots of action - excited neighbours popping in and out with lots of talk and tears, yes, even in front of the children. It was quite frightening for we had never seen grown-ups act like this before. No-one seemed to know what they were supposed to do. Although we had been expecting war for a long time, when it did come it was still a shock. It just didn't seem real - it made us feel so helpless and stunned to think we had been powerless to divert it.

England was now at war. This war was eventually to involve the whole world. This war, even though we didn't know it at the time, was going to last five years, eight months and four days and it was to target every man, woman and child. Hitler aimed for the young, the not-so-young and the old.

From that day in September our lives were to be turned upside down. We were introduced to a life of shortages, ration books, air-raid shelters, bombs, death, separation, evacuation, tears and sadness.

We were taught to have a deadly hate for our foe and a fearless love for our country. We all became very patriotic: everything was for our King and country - King George VI, Defender of the Faith, Keeper of the Peace, King of England and Ireland and the British dominions beyond the seas; Emperor of India. Yes. we were a proud nation.

V . . . —

V . . . —

Chapter One - Rosie

I was six years old when the Second World War started and living in Finsbury Park. It was just an ordinary day for such a big thing to happen. Although, I must admit, war didn't mean much to us children at the time. It was just a word we had heard rather a lot of and it seemed to us children to be a grown-up thing. Bill and I never imagined it would alter our lives in any way. We just wanted to go out for our Sunday stroll with Mum and Dad as we usually did.

A stroll was my dad's word for a long leisurely walk. Most Sundays it was a walk along the Thames Embankment. Other times we went to the Sunday markets; that was when Dad needed tools to repair the house or a piece of leather to repair the shoes. You could buy anything in these markets. They even sold animals - poor little dogs and cats.

One man we knew would go around all the markets selling his own dog. As soon as the new owner let the dog off the leash, it was off like the wind, back to its master. Then he would sell it again the next week. This went on for some time until in the end the man got caught and was stopped from selling animals, especially his own dog. Ha-ha! It did cause a laugh.

Bill and I felt sad for the poor animals. But we did like all the hustle and bustle and all the haggling in the street markets, like Brick Lane, Petticoat Lane, Bethnal Green, the Roman Road and Spitafields, in the East End, Chapel Street in Islington, and Ridley Road in Dalston. On special occasions there would be a Pearly King and Queen in the market. They

1

would be collecting money for some charity. I loved the way they dressed with all the pearl buttons sewn on to their clothes. It looked so pretty. Pearly Kings and Queens had to be real Cockneys - that's people born within the sound of the Bow Bells.

Mum didn't come with us on these trips to market; she didn't like the crowds so she stayed home to cook our dinner.

People's time was more organised in those days. We had set times for everything - breakfast, dinner, tea and supper - and also set meals for certain days. Thus our Sunday strolls or Sunday outings were part of our ritual. Hitler was not going to stop that. How could he? We were soon to find out that he could and it was not long before we found out how. But, for the time being, life was to carry on as usual and we kids still went out for our Sunday outings; we looked forward to them and we loved them.

Going for a stroll

After our breakfast, on most summer Sundays Dad would say, "Put on your best bib and tucker, kids, we're going out for a stroll." We would quickly put on our best Sunday clothes and go to catch the bus at Finsbury Park station. This was a red double-decker trolley-bus; it would take us to Kings Cross, where we would change to another bus that would take us to the Embankment.

We would get off this bus just before Blackfriars Bridge near the Smithfield Meat Market. (That was where my granddad had worked as a Meat Porter before he died. Granddad died in hospital after being hit over the head by another patient. Granddad died when I was three years old.)

The reason we got off the bus here was simply this: if we got off the Clerkenwell side of the bridge it gave us a choice: **one**, we could walk down the road to see St Paul's Cathedral, as there was always something going on there; or **two**, we could go up Fleet Street and see the Royal Courts of Justice and all the busy newspaper offices. I know it will seem terribly boring to people nowadays but it wasn't then as there were lots of things going on. You could always see the VIPs (very important people) who you would never have seen if you hadn't gone there to look for them. (You only looked - you wouldn't dare talk to them.)

2

As you know, there was no TV in 1939, at least not for the ordinary people. **Three**, we could go down onto the Embankment and watch the boats on the River Thames. That was my favourite. It was lovely there. I loved the river; I could have stayed there all day.

Old Father Thames

I liked to sit on the wall by Cleopatra's Needle and dream of all the wealth and the piracy that had taken place on the Thames in days gone by - River Pirates, Night Plunderers and the Mud Larks, things we had learnt at school and things we had seen for ourselves in the old pirate tunnels under the docks. My dad said I was a dreamer.

The River Thames was used a lot in those days. We called it "Old Father Thames" after the song about it: "Old Father Thames keeps rolling along down to the mighty sea," which it does, and of course, it was going to be famous again very soon, owing to the war.

At that time, though, we would spend all day out. Our mum would take a picnic which we would eat by the river; then we would go to look at all the important places in that part of London. Our mum and dad wanted us to know all about our town's famous places and its history.

After we had eaten we would walk the full length of the Embankment. We would then come to the Houses of Parliament and Big Ben. There we would have a lecture on the government and how they should run the country, or at least according to Harry Wright, my dad. I thought he was very clever. We would never leave the Embankment until Big Ben had chimed. We always waited for that, otherwise we felt we hadn't seen him. We felt so proud of our clock because you could hear it on the wireless and it was known all over the world.

Soap-box

At other times we would go to St James's Park and Buckingham Palace. I liked Hyde Park best. It was much more fun as my dad always made a "bee-line" for "Speakers' Corner"; that's where people would stand on a "soap-box" and air their views mostly about religion and politics.

Dad loved a good argument and politics was his favourite subject. He would stand and heckle some speaker, disagreeing with everything the poor man said - that is if he didn't have the same ideas as my dad. Sometimes it nearly came to blows.

When my dad had his turn on the soap-box though, it was quite a different story. He didn't like it when he was being heckled. My dad could dish it out but didn't like it when he got it back. Unfortunately we always missed the best parts because my mum always took us away with the excuse of feeding the ducks on the Serpentine, saying, "Leave him alone he's enjoying himself." I have even seen my dad come back with a black eye and I have heard my mum say, "Good job, that's for opening your big gob." Dad would say he was "right by name and right by nature." That would make everyone spitting mad and bring everyone to the verge of giving him a bloody nose. Dad could be very aggravating.

Up the park

My mum and dad liked taking me to the parks because people liked me, especially the tourists (Americans). They liked me because I was a cheeky little Cockney Kid and I was fortunate enough to be pretty as well; otherwise I might not have got away with all my cheek. I think I was already developing the big gob. (A bit of the old man coming out.) "They say the apple doesn't fall far from the tree."

These American tourists always gave me money for sweets, which my mum quickly took off me saying they were foreign coins.

(No wonder I grew up quickly.) With the money they had given me, she would buy fish and chips for us all, which we ate on the way home out of the newspaper it was wrapped in. It was delicious. I have never tasted fish and chips like it since. (I suppose the newspaper print is different these days.)

Mum also bought herself two penny-worth of crackling (bits of batter that come off the fish while it was frying) It is considered very bad for you today. Doctors would have a fit if you ate anything like that now, but ignorance is bliss and it was nice and tasty. Alas, times change and things were to become very different. We now had a war on our hands, thanks to Adolph Hitler, and our strolls were to become a thing of the past.

Wednesday's child

I was born in London in a place called Islington on the 9th of August 1933. At this time England was in the midst of a deep depression. I was born in a sweltering heat wave of ninety degrees Fahrenheit (thirty-two degrees Centigrade). I was named Rosie. At the time of my arrival into this confused, worried and hungry world, my parents were living, "blissfully happy", in two rooms over a shop in Story Street, just off the Caledonian Road. It was right by the biggest Friday market in all of London - the Caledonian Road cattle market.

This market had 2,000 stalls which were put around the empty cattle pens; these pens were used by the cattle auctioneers on their market days, Monday to Thursday. On these days over 7,000 bulls and cattle were sold. The cattle market was also an abattoir. It also handled thousands of sheep, pigs and horses.

It was a strange sight seeing these frightened animals being driven down the "Cali" from the cattle trains by the drovers. The bellowing of the bulls and the yelling of the drovers didn't seem to fit very well into Islington. It was more like the "Wild West". You would have expected to see someone like John Wayne. The cattle market closed in 1939 because of the war and so did the Friday market. The abattoir stayed for much longer.

In 1933, when I was born, my dad was unemployed as most of the men were at that time. Dad was a cabinet maker - a wood machinist, a highly skilled profession. Nevertheless there was no work to be found for him anywhere. So Mum and Dad decided that Dad should stay home to look after me while Mum went out to work. My mum already had a job, she was a waitress at the St Pancras Hotel, Kings Cross. She had chosen to work in a hotel rather than go into service. Most young

5

girls in my mum's day did go into service to become servants for the posh, rich people.

My mum would not have liked being a servant. Life in those days was just the same as it is today: rich and poor. I suppose it will always be the same; nothing will ever change, at least not until there is a fairer distribution of money. But how do you do that?

Poverty-stricken

At this time there was also a lot of unrest. There was mass unemployment throughout the country and the poorest families had no money at all. They were not even able to buy food for themselves or for their children. The people were literally starving to death. Babies and young children were dying from hunger. You had to take what was called a means test before you were entitled to get any help from the government.

A means test meant you had to have nothing left that you could sell or possess anything you could call your own. You had to be "poverty stricken".

This was unacceptable; what could they means test them on? They had nothing. There was no work; there was no money, therefore no food. Families were dying. What more proof did the government want?

Hunger marches were organised from all over the country. The marchers were to walk to London and meet in Hyde Park to have a confrontation with the government and let the politicians know what they needed and expected from them.

The hunger marchers chanted as they walked, "Down with the means test. We want bread." As you can imagine, as always happens, the police stepped in and there were "clashes" with them as there always are.

The outcome of the marches was that the government promised to take an urgent look into their unemployment policies, although only a short time later it all happened again. It took a world war to get this all sorted out.

Meanwhile Hitler and his Nazi party were goose-stepping all over Germany, winning elections and wooing the young people. He had formed what was known as the Hitler Youth and the Hitler Maidens. He dissolved the Boy Scouts, making all young German boys join the Hitler Youth organisation.

There was no stopping him. England at this time was too bogged down in her own depression and just watched. We were mesmerised by his cheek. We were powerless to do anything about what he was doing.

Hitlerism was being born. It was not going to be too long before we were going to hear a lot more of Herr Hitler's hissing and rasping voice and see his Nazi salute and swastika arm bands.

We were to see him and his Storm Troopers goose-step all over Europe, causing World War II. In the meantime, while all this was going on and war was definitely in the air, I was dragged kicking and screaming into this uneasy world - on a Wednesday, would you believe? "Wednesday's" child is full of woe."

New house, new baby

About a year after my birth, my parents decided it was time to move from the Cali, as, by now, this flat in Story Street was getting too small for the three of us. Mum soon found us another house in which to live; it was at Finsbury Park. The problem was: how were we going to move our furniture to the new house? Dad had a bright idea and went to ask Charley the coster-monger if we could borrow his barrow. Charley agreed to let Dad have the barrow for a few hours and even helped to load our furniture on it (for a fee). My dad had to push that loaded barrow all the way up the Caledonian Road, past the Nags Head, up Seven Sisters Road to Finsbury Park, to our new place in St Thomas's Street.

Mum and I went by bus. We had now moved into St Thomas's Street right next to the Finsbury Park Empire. That was a well-known Music Hall where famous stars did their shows. My mum liked the Music Hall and so did I. As I grew older she took me with her to see the shows and even though I was very young, I still remember seeing Frankie Howard doing his fishes song. He was so funny. Mum laughed until she cried. Alas, the Finsbury Park Empire was pulled down after the war; it is now a block of flats.

After successfully rearing me for a few years, my parents decided they were qualified to give me a little brother or sister.

I can vaguely recall not liking the idea very much but I soon got used to it and in due time I acquired a little brother. He was named William. We called him Bill for short.

Bill was a big, fat, wobbly dumpling of a baby. I loved him. He would call me "Wosie". He was such a lovely little boy. I ask my mum if we could have another one.

Dad laughed and said he couldn't afford any more; he had spent all his money buying us two. Mum said she was quite happy with her "Pigeon Pair". I still kept asking though, until Mum gave me a dig in the ribs and told me to shut up.

The Arsenal FC

As I grew older I went with my dad to watch the Arsenal Football Club play. My dad was an Arsenal fanatic. The Arsenal Football Stadium was not far from our house. It only took a five minute walk along the Blackstock road to get there. Dad sometimes had to carry me there on his shoulders as I was only a little tiddler and would soon get lost in the crowds. The Arsenal always had a lot of supporters and people would stream in from all directions. The nearest station was Gillespie Road tube station, changed in 1932 to Arsenal Station at the request of Herbert Chapman, Arsenal's manager at that time.

When we were inside the grounds and the game was on, if I couldn't see the game properly I would say, "Come on Dad, give me a flying angel," and he would hoist me up on his shoulders again and I would be towering above everyone at the match, as my dad was rather tall. Dad sold programmes at the Arsenal Football Ground. He soon sold out and we always saw the whole match. We always stood at the North Bank. That was the most exciting place to be. If the "Gunners" lost we could not speak to Dad for the rest of the day. Mum would know the result of the match by looking at Dad's face when he came home.

Cod-liver oil & malt

I started at St Thomas's school at four years old. I was given malt, milk, cod-liver oil and orange juice because they said I was too thin and underfed (cheek!). I liked the malt and orange juice but hated the milk and cod-liver oil. The milk was full cream and came in gills, one gill bottle for each child.

8

One gill equalled a quarter of a pint. This milk was freezing in the winter with lumps of ice in it or too warm and full of grease in the summer. Whichever way it came, it made me feel sick. I never did like milk.

By the time Bill started school, I was malt and vitamin monitor. I used to make him line up with the other kids to get some malt even though he didn't need it because he was fat enough. If others had to suffer with that stuff, then so should he. It was a case of being cruel to be kind. I used to make him come around twice for the malt, with a great big tablespoon. He didn't like it; it made him gag. I used to laugh. He used to cry and tell my mum but she didn't mind because she thought it was a good idea for him to have some if it made him strong. The Headmaster asked me why my tin of malt ran out so quickly; I just said that I had more children in my queue. He left it at that. I don't think he really wanted to know. I used to watch his face as great dollops of malt went into children's mouths; he used to shudder.

Schooldays are...?

St Thomas's School was just like all the other schools, cold and miserable in the winter, and hot and miserable in the summer. We only had a concrete square for a playground. I hated play-time. I could not understand why we children had to go out into the playground in the freezing cold winter, while our teacher stayed in the school. We had to stay outside for twenty minutes. It seemed more like twenty years. It was no better in our classrooms; they were very cold and we had to keep our hats, coats and gloves on at times.

In class we sat two at a desk, in rows facing the front. That was where our teacher stood writing things on the blackboard and occasionally turning around and glaring at us, in case we were up to something. I was positive that woman had eyes in the back of her head, as she always caught me doing something: "Rosie Wright!" Go and stand in the corner." I didn't mind, I liked it. I was such a show-off. If the other children encouraged me enough I would stand there pulling faces. That would make them laugh which got me into more trouble.

In school we didn't use pencil and paper. We had slate boards and chalk. The chalk sent your teeth on edge if it scraped across the slate at a funny angle. It also made your fingers sore when the chalk was nearly finished. It was not until you got into your higher classes that you graduated to pencil and paper, then, much later, to pen and ink. Ink came in ink-wells. Pens had nibs. What a mess you got yourself into when you first started to use them.

Bells ruled our life in school - they rang for everything: in-time, out-time, play-time, lunch-time and home-time. That was the best one of all: home-time. Bill and I were attending St Thomas's School when World War II started.

V . . . —

Chapter Two - The First Evacuation - 1939

The Government decided to close the schools. It was decreed that all children and pregnant women should be evacuated out of London and all other densely populated places. So a mass evacuation plan went into action. The children had to be got out of London and other cities throughout England as soon as possible. There was to be a mass exodus to the country, to a place of safety, as no-one knew what to expect. There had never been any previous experience of a world war involving cities and towns and, worst of all, the targeting civilians. And now this war was going to involve aircraft and poison gas.

The schools helped to evacuate the children. It was decided that parents would have to take the children to their own school. There they would wait with them until the bus came to take them to the train station; then on to a place of safety. Mothers had to tie labels with their name and address on it to their children's coat buttons so they would not get lost in all the confusion. Mothers tearfully waved their children goodbye at the school gates, not even knowing where they were going. Then came the agonising wait for the parents while their children were being billeted out.

The children were only allowed to take their gas-mask, some spare clothes, a toothbrush (if you had one), and a comb plus a bag of food to get you through that day. This was a terrible time for the families. It was a very sad and unhappy time for the children. We had been taken away from our homes. We were frightened and bewildered. What was happening? First our dad gets "called up" and then goes away. Then we are sent away. What would happen next?

Our lives were turned upside down. Our only thought was, what will happen to our mum without us? Who will look after her? Our hearts were breaking. Some of the children were sobbing. It was a sad and miserable time. Hitler had a lot to answer for.

When we children arrived at our destination the people from the village came out to have a look at us and if they liked how we look they would say: "I'll have that one." We were all a sorry sight - miserable little kids, missing our mums and dads and only wanting to be home. We were tired from the journey and all the hanging around. We were also hungry now because we had eaten our bag of food for that day.

When eventually I was chosen, I informed the lady, "You can't have me unless my brother comes along too, as I have to look after him. My mum said so." The people who took us into their homes were paid about ten shillings a week and they were given the blankets for our beds. It was not a lot but I supposed it helped, although it didn't make things any easier for us because their children didn't like us. They called us "townies" when they were being "friendly" and "rotten filthy Londoners" and "bomb dodgers" when they were being cruel.

When the foster families took us into their homes, we were put straight into a bath of hot soapy water. The London children thought they were being murdered. There was a terrible fuss, as most of us had never been in a real bath before. In London we could only have what was called "a wash down". This was done in a small bowl of water. Most houses in London had no water inside the house. You had to go outside to the water tap in the yard to get some, then you had to heat it on the kitchen range. It took ages to get hot enough. So we were very economical.

It took a week before I could tell my mum where we were and give her our new address. Our group from Finsbury Park had landed up in Hertfordshire.

Hertfordshire had been allocated about 85,000 evacuee children. Some of our friends went to Wolverhampton. Lots of children went to Cornwall, Scotland and Wales. Children were evacuated all over Britain. Later, some children were even sent to Canada and Australia; that was the second evacuation (the result of the Blitz on London and the pending invasion of England when everything was pointing to Hitler winning the war). My brother Bill and I were two of those miserable kids sent off to the country for our safety, although we didn't want to go. I told my mum I was going to run away but she made me promise to look after my brother Bill.

I was six years old, with the mind of a grandmother and the vocabulary of a trooper. I wrote to my mum several times asking her to come and bring us home. I told her we didn't like it there. We hated the countryside.

I knew if I told her Billy was making himself ill with fretting for her she would come down right away to see him. So I wrote and said he was. After a month Mum did come to visit us and when she went back to London, we both came back with her.

London blacks out

We came home to a very different London. By now there was total black-out. All windows were covered with black-out material made into curtains. These thick black curtains prevented all light from showing. The ARP wardens were very strict about this. If there was an air-raid on and you showed even a chink of light, the air-raid warden would come around and shout: "Put that blooming light out." Because even a small light could alert a German bomber. You were not even allowed to light a fag in the street during a raid because you could put everyone's life in danger. People who kept offending had to pay a hefty fine and face the anger of their neighbours.

By now the street lamp-lighter had disappeared from our streets, never to be seen again because after the war the street lights were electric. But for now he had most likely been called up into the forces - fighting for his country.

For us children though, it all seemed very exciting - no street lights, just creeping about in the dark, nearly getting run over by cars and buses you could hardly see. Car lights were either covered with cardboard, with a cross cut out, or painted with black paint, with a spot left clear. Thus the little light they did show would only give you a glimpse of the white lines on the curbs and lamp-posts. It would also pick out the new invention, reflector studs, all down the middle of the road. These were called "Cat's eyes."

Last but not least, this speck of light would be seen by the pedestrians. Some car owners even painted their tyres white so the public could see them in the dark. Buses, trains and shops had sticky criss-cross tape over their windows to protect you from the risk of shattered glass. Petrol was about nine pence a gallon at this time. But most people didn't have a car, or the nine pence.

To top it all we imagined that we saw Germans everywhere. Everyone was talking in whispers about spies and saying things like: " Careless talk costs lives"; "Walls have ears"; "Be like Dad, keep mum." (Oops! - to "keep mum" only means to keep quiet, not to talk too much. We must be politically correct today).

There were big posters all over the place telling us not to gossip, not to waste, not to spread rumours - but to work, dig and save all in the aid of victory. We had to work in the factories, dig in our gardens and allotments and grow our own food. We had to save our money and buy war bonds and save our pennies weekly, to make a salute the forces. Up to this point no bombs had been dropped on England.

Our air-raid shelters

Bill and I were glad to be home and, as time passed, more and more children came home from evacuation. Some schools had to be opened again, but for now, we children were enjoying ourselves with all our new-found freedom. Still nothing much was happening. It was now being called "The phoney war".

The sirens would go and we would all show a clean pair of heels and dive into the nearest air-raid shelter; then, almost immediately, the all-clear would sound and we would all come out again. In the end the people just ignored the warnings and fell into a sense of false security. It all seemed like a big joke. We all thought it was funny. It was easy to get into the air-raid shelters as the shelters were built in every street. They were built down one side of the road with their entrances facing the curb and the houses.

They were low, re-enforced brick buildings with built-in bunk beds and they were very sparse on comfort. These bunk beds were for the night-time raids when people would have to sleep in the shelters. They would have to bring their own bedding and any comfort that might be needed. It was not going to be too long before we would be glad to use these shelters, even though they were to prove freezing cold and terribly damp in the winter, and hot and smelly in the summer.

There was no light in these shelters, so along with our mattresses, blankets, hot water bottles and flasks of tea we would have to bring torches, matches, candles or night lights.

No old person was to be left alone in his or her house when a raid was on, and a neighbour or a warden would go to get them. I believe some old people almost enjoyed these false alarms just for the company. Our mums were lonely too, as by now most of our dads had been called up and mixing in company and looking after each other was good for us all.

As the time passed we started to think these little raids were all we were going to get and that the war would soon be over. The government had said that the war would be over by Christmas.

They were wrong. (What's new?) But we must give credit where it's due, they didn't say which Christmas.

People were beginning to think the German planes couldn't reach Britain. It was a happy thought but it wasn't to be too long before we found out they could.

In the meantime we kids had marvellous games. We had a big family, we all lived near each other. All our cousins and friends were home again now and there was quite a gang of us. Things were changing. Our dads and uncles were all away on active service in foreign lands while our mums were working in the ammunition factories. My mum and her sisters went to work in the Ever-ready factory which had made batteries before the war, as well as Cossers who made wirelesses. Both these factories had been commandeered to make ammunition. A call had gone out for 100,000 women to work around the clock in ammunition factories throughout Britain in a war effort to keep our troops fully armed. The women took up the challenge and three times that number signed on. These factories were never closed.

Ghosties, witches & long-legged beasties

We children were mostly left to our own devices. Our Nana looked after Bill and me with the help of my Auntie Elsie as we were always in her house.

My Auntie Elsie had a big family and an extremely big house in Highbury Quadrant which looked like a mansion. This house was very old and was tall, with lots of windows, all shuttered up to protect people from shattered glass if a bomb dropped nearby.

The front of the house was always dark even in summer. There were two big gnarled old oak trees growing in the front garden that robbed the house of any light. We used to call then "hanging trees" and "witches trees" to frighten the younger ones. It looked very eerie in the dark and was seriously creepy at the best of times but it was a lovely house to explore with all its rooms and passages.

We had wonderful games in that great big ghostly old house. Most of the rooms were unoccupied so we would play hide and seek in them. We would scare the life out of each other and run screaming through floor after floor of empty rooms terrified, with our hair standing up on the backs of our necks with pure fear. We would be almost hysterical with uncontrolled laughter. We could almost see the ghost that was after us, we could feel it breathing down our necks. It would scare the living daylights out of us, just the sheer terror of something that was going to grab us.

We had wonderful times there in the early days of the war. No-one ever complained or stopped us from playing but things were soon going to change.

Mrs Wiseman

Mrs Wiseman lived alone in the basement flat of this house and was hardly ever seen by anyone. We older children told the younger ones she was a ghost. It was just to frighten them and make them be our slaves. We would frighten them into doing anything we wanted with the threat of calling Mrs W. If they disobeyed us in any way we would wave our arms in the air and say: "Woo-woo where are you, Mrs W?" The younger ones believed she would appear so they would do anything we asked them to. Mrs W! She didn't seem to mind us lot running amok through the house yelling, screaming and laughing. Then, one day, one of the younger ones was caught by my Auntie Elsie while he was carrying out our orders. (Our orders usually involved nicking food from Auntie's larder.) She ask him what he was doing and he told her he was a slave and if he didn't do as he was told Mrs W would get him. After that the fat was really in the fire. Auntie Elsie went berserk.

We were all frog marched down to Mrs W's flat to apologise to her. Mrs W must have wondered what was wrong as she was quite oblivious to it all. She took no notice of what was going on and lived in a world of her own. Mrs W was a little Jewish lady. She was really very nice. Auntie Elsie locked the larder and we were made to feel thoroughly ashamed of ourselves. Later on, as the war progressed, Mrs W went to live with her daughter and the basement flat was taken over by the airforce while a barrage balloon was put on the tennis courts behind the house.

The quadrant

All of the neighbours and friends were Jewish. Highbury Quadrant was a Jewish area. Sabina and Pamela were two of our friends who lived in the Quadrant. They were my cousin's friends more than mine.

I got to know them by going around with my cousin Kathy Bailey to their houses on a Friday night at sundown and turning out their lamps and doing odd jobs that they were not allowed to do until Sunday.

On Saturdays we had to pay the milkman, the coalman and anyone who needed paying that day; we also had to do any jobs that needed doing. We would light their fires for them and pop in several times during the day to stoke up the fire and see if anything else needed to be done. These people were very pleased with us and they were very good to us. Whenever they had a feast day we were allowed to go to it. They told us just to get on and eat and not to worry about their praying which seemed to be after every mouthful. We didn't need telling twice. We had never tasted food like that before. It was delicious - not like ours which was fish paste, Bully Beef, or Spam and things we had grown ourselves in the back garden, in an effort to dig for victory. That was my war effort, not just growing it but eating it. I grew radishes and my brother grew turnips; both were like rubber and riddled with maggots and slugs.

Our money and rations

By now things were rapidly changing. Ration books were more important than money. Rationing came in on the 1st January 1940: we were not to know it would last for the next fourteen years. It finally finished in 1953.

It was a fair rationing system, each man, woman and child was entitled to their fair share. It controlled profiteering by the "spivs" and it controlled the price in the shops. You could not control the black market although ordinary families couldn't afford black market prices.

Our rations were meagre but fed us. They kept body and soul together. I can't remember ever being starving hungry, just hungry like kids always are. Some poor people had never eaten so well.

For many of the poorer families rationing introduced more protein and vitamins. The diet was very much like what the doctors would like us to eat today: low fat, low salt, low sugar, high fibre.

School dinners were introduced during the war so that schoolchildren could have the best possible main meal of the day at lunch-time. This would be a great help to their mothers, who were out working long hours for the war effort in the ammunition factories. They would return home from work, too late to cook a meal. Most people were employed now and had money to spend but there was nothing to spend it on.

This is an idea of what our rations were.

8 oz sugar every four weeks.
8 oz fat every four weeks (only 2 oz could be butter);
    the other 6 oz were for cooking purposes
2 oz tea every week
2 oz cheese every four weeks

18

3 pints of milk per week, sometimes dropping to 2 pints
1 packet of dried milk every four weeks
4 oz of bacon (meat was rationed by price: 1/2d per
head and 2d of that had to spent on corned beef.)
1 egg in its shell per month per person.

We still had plenty of bread at this time. Bread was our mainstay; it filled us up. We had what was called the national loaf. It was grey and stodgy but we didn't mind. Some of my favourite ways of eating bread were dipping it in a cup of hot Oxo or eating Marmite sandwiches; that was the best way to eat bread if you had used all your butter ration up.

I loved toast and dripping, that was a real treat. We would take a slice of bread and stick it on a fork and hold it up to the fire and keep it there until it was toasted. The bread tasted lovely and smoky from the coal fire. (It would probably kill us today.) The dripping was made from any kind of meat you could get. With this meat Mum usually made two meals.

First, she would boil it with some vegetables and pearl barley; this was made into a vegetable broth for us kids. We hated it. Then, with the same piece of meat, Mum would put it in a dish, in the oven with some water, herbs and cooking lard and roast it. This was for another meal; the juice from the water and lard made the dripping. It was lovely. I also loved bread and condensed milk but I wasn't allowed to have it as it was used for the tea - it acted as both milk and sweetener. It took a lot of points from your ration book.

Later, the size of the national loaf was cut, then that to went on ration: two big loafs a week for an adult and one for each child. We were looking hunger in the eye without our bread.

There were always plenty of vegetables. People who had been blessed with green fingers were able to grow their vegetables in their gardens. If they had grown too many, they would sell them or give them away to their neighbours.

Later we had to have powdered potatoes, powdered eggs, powdered milk. Then even soap went on ration. Bill said he was glad as now he wouldn't have to wash so often. Offal, rabbit and game were "off coupons". We still had a lot of fish; I believe some of it was shark.

It was in those far off days of World War II that Spam was invented. Spam is chopped pork and ham - S P A M (supply pressed American meat). It came from America. Trust the yanks. (Good old Uncle Sam.) Spam could be served hot, cold or fried. I liked it best fried. It wasn't too bad, not like some of the stuff the government tried on us. It's hard to imagine that a lot of people in those days had only five pounds a week to live on - that was to pay everything with. Rent was about five shillings or ten shillings per week. Gas was approximately one penny per night. Food, clothes and fuel soon took the rest.

Food was the biggest outlay. How much was spent on it depended on what was in the shops. Not many houses had electricity. I didn't know anyone who had electricity at that time.

Gas lit the houses. The gas came into the house from underground pipes from the Gas Works (where the coal gas is manufactured). The gas came into the house to a gas meter into which you put your money. It then fed a hooked pipe/bracket on the wall which was your light. Onto this pipe/bracket you put a very delicate white membrane. You then turned it on and put a lighted match to it. It made a hissing sound all the time it was on.

These gas mantles didn't last very long. They cost a penny each and you could get them in any Oil shop or in Woolworth.

The postman

The post would be delivered four times a day and on Sundays. The last delivery of the day was at four o'clock in the afternoon. It was nothing like the way it is today and the postman would be waited for in the hope of letters being brought from husband, sons and daughters away fighting in other countries.

The postman was our friend. On the other hand the telegram boy was one to dread. He stuck terror into the hearts of the women as he cycled down the street. The telegram boy was always the bearer of bad news. The telegrams were always from the War Office with news of someone's husband, son or daughter missing in action or known to be killed in action.

People would hold their breath until he had passed them and knocked on the door of some other unfortunate house. These were sad times but we shared each others grief and sorrow. People were very supportive of each other. We all needed each other so much and each neighbour's bad news was our bad news also.

Every night the newspaper boy would come around our street shouting, "La de da, come and get your la de da [cockney slang for the *Star* newspaper]."

We also had the vinegar man who would come around with his big vats of vinegar on his horse and cart and from whom you bought your vinegar by the pint. There was the salt man's horse and cart too, with his great blocks of salt which he cut to the size you wanted.

Then there was the man with the seafood barrow. We kids called him the "Winkle man". He sold his winkles and shrimps by the pint. He also sold cockles, mussels and crabs.

These coster-mongers always had a cheerful word and a joke. They would cheer us up and make us laugh. They would let us kids help them.

These men were all called up into the fighting forces. Food got scarce and rationing really took hold. Gone was the cheerful cockney fruit and veg man ("Have a Jaffa Gaffa") from whom you could buy a tuppenny orange or a penny apple. All the traders disappeared from our streets.

At about this time oranges vanished from our shops and stalls; we never saw them again until after the war. We never saw a banana all through the war. When they did came back after the war, the young children who had never seen a banana tried to eat them with the skins on.

DIY

We had no social security, no family allowance, no NHS. It cost 7/6 to call your doctor out so, as you can imagine, we didn't see much of him. My nana cured us all with her home-made remedies. It's a wonder we have lived to tell the tale.

I still shudder at the thought of drinking hot peppermint for a tummy ache or drinking hot Senna-pod tea and that disgusting stuff, "Cascara", or taking big spoonfuls of syrup of figs - all to make you go. It sure did! What with the horrible smell of the Camphorated Oil that was rubbed on your neck and chest when you had a cold and the way it lingered on your thermogene vest or liberty bodice for weeks, it's a wonder anyone would get near us.

When we had whooping cough we were marched around the streets coughing and wheezing until we found out where the workmen were mending the roads with tar. Then we would have to stand there breathing the tar fumes into our lungs. You would find most of your friends there having to do the same thing. We would grumble but no-one ever considered our feelings; we were just told to shut up. It was for our own good.

The classic remedy for the earache was a baked onion: take out the middle, poke it in your ear and tie it up with a piece of white cloth or red flannel. There was also the piping hot bread poultice applied to your boil—it was inhuman. It was better to say nothing and suffer in silence.

All these things worked though and did make us better though I suspect it was our nana's TLC (tender loving care) that did it really.

Our nana was a pretty lady. She had lovely long, black, curly hair which she wore in a bun and very dark, brown, kind eyes. She always wore dangling ear-rings. Nana was a very kind person, just like my mum. Nana took good care of us and helped to keep us fed, clean and tidy while Mum was at work.

Our shops

During the war you had to "register" with certain shops. You could not shop in any store you fancied - it had to be the one that was most convenient to you. You had to register with a grocer and a reputable butcher in order to get your fair share of the goodies that were on offer from time to time and, of course, to get what was rightfully yours.

You had to register with a reputable butcher because it was best to know your butcher and be able to trust him as there were some scams going on. When a butcher put a notice in his shop window saying "Rabbits for Sale" you had to know he was telling the truth.

When a notice went up that there was some offal for sale the word soon got around and queues would form quickly. Goodness knows how the grapevine worked but it did, and you had to be quick, though of course, not everyone was lucky.

We would all rush to queue up to get whatever was going. If ever a queue formed we would just join it, as there was bound to have been something we wanted. The truth was that we wanted more or less everything so it didn't matter what was on sale. At long last we had some money but there was nothing much to spend it on. The war, no matter how bad it was, was putting money into the pockets of the ordinary people. While my mum was at work, I was in charge of the shopping. Nana wasn't "pushy" enough so Mum said I should do it instead. I was quite street-wise and knew what to buy. I knew I should never, ever, buy a rabbit without its head and tail on as it might be a cat, given that a cat and a rabbit look very much alike minus their head and tail.

My mum would be over the moon if she came home from work to a piece of liver and some kidneys. That was a rare treat for Mum and Dad too if he was home on leave but we kids didn't like offal. I can still see my dad sitting at the table, looking at his dinner, smacking his lips and saying, "Cor!" Then he would quickly eat it all up.

You didn't have to register with a greengrocer as veg was not on rations. In our local greengrocer at Easter time we would buy day-old chicks for a penny each. They were lovely fluffy yellow chicks which soon died in spite of us keeping them warm on our kitchen range. Bill and I always landed up in floods of tears. The chicks were always ceremoniously buried in our backyard with Bill and I providing a full burial service. I sang hymns. Mum stopped us from buying them. I don't know if it was because we were always so upset when they died or if it was my singing. Besides, we were running out of empty space in our yard for this sort of thing.

Coupons

In those days we were always having to make do. We were fed up with it. People were always running out of things, that's when the borrowing started. "You can tell the borrowers," Mum said. I never worked that one out. How can you tell who was and who wasn't? Mum would tell me I should be observant.

Neighbours would borrow cups of sugar, some tea, a few slices of bread and some butter, anything. These things were all to be returned on the next month's food rations. But, by the time the next month came around and provided they had paid you back, it all started again. So it went on. Some people sold their coupons. They were not allowed to and you were not allowed to buy them, but people did so nevertheless. Bill and I never went without much. I know mum and nana went without a few nice things so that we children could have them.

For instance, we would have all our mums' and our nanas' sweet coupons, since we would soon run out of our own. But we did share our sweets with my mum and nana. Mum loved coconut ice. Nana loved Palm toffees. I liked Tom Thumb drops because they lasted longer. I also liked treacle toffee and gob-stoppers. Bill liked Fry's Chocolate bars and jelly babies.

He would make what was called German snot with his jelly babies. This was made by chewing a jelly baby, then mixing it up in the middle of his hand until it was a gooey mess. It would make me feel sick. You needed 2 Es or 4 Ds coupons for a quarter of sweets. They were cut out of your ration book. You were allowed twelve ounces of sweets every four weeks.

You had to buy two ounces at a time. Your coupons soon ran out and you had to wait until the next month before you got any more, unless, of course, you could scrounge them from any of your aunties or uncles. But then you were always made to do some job for them, usually the worst job they could think of or one they hated doing the most. Cleaning the shoes was the worst or putting blanko on the plimsolls. It took ages and you got yourself in such a mess.

You needed clothes coupons to buy shoes, clothes or material and the young girls never had enough of them. The clothes in the shops were pretty ordinary and were called "utility" clothes. They had been made with less material so that less work had to be done on them. Being very basic, they had no pockets or any fancy trimmings and they were put together very quickly, leaving the women seamstresses free to work in the ammunition factories as compulsory part-timers. Some of the girls made their own clothes out of blackout material which was left over after the regulation blackout curtains were made. Others used parachute silk from the firm who made the parachutes and sold as offcuts. These dresses were better than those sold in the shops. My mum had a dress made for me from our left-over blackout curtain material.

Fashion was on ration. If a young girl wanted to get married in white, it was net curtain material and butter muslin that would be used for her dress and veil. But a bride always managed to look lovely on her wedding day. The bridegrooms were mostly in uniform. Old curtains which were no longer needed for the windows were made into nighties and pyjamas or anything else that might be needed. If there was any material that was silky it was made into underclothes. Girls were very inventive in the war days.

As to men's fashion, well, there isn't much to say about men's fashion. It seemed to me that most men wore a hat: there was the pork-pie hat, the sort worn by the comedian Tony Hancock and my uncle Fred. There was the bowler hat, the sort worn by the tipsters at the dog or horse tracks. Then there was the cap, the kind worn by Andy Capp, the beer-swilling, fag-smoking, football-loving, husband of poor Florrie Capp, and the working man's favourite hat. Then there was the Trilby. This hat was worn by gangsters and detectives. I think the Trilby was the best hat of them all and it was worn by my dad.

Little boys always wore a cap, along with short grey trousers down to their knees and long grey socks up to their knees, a white shirt, a tie and a pullover. This style never changed summer or winter.

There wasn't much fashion for the man in the street in those days. They were too poor to buy clothes for themselves before the war and now that they had some money they were in uniform. Things did get a bit better later but not before the disaster of the "demob" suit.

Make do and mend

Housewives' lives were centred round the ration book. Once again we had to make do and mend. Mums had to darn their children's socks, disastrous but we all had to make sacrifices. There's many a blister I've cursed Hitler for. I would rather have gone around with "Taters" (holes) in my socks than let my mum mend them. It was okay when nana mended them. Nana knew how to darn.

Collars and cuffs on shirts and blouses, had to be turned when they wore out or became frayed. My mum was no good at that sort of thing. Dad called her sewing "dogs' teeth". She couldn't even sew a button on. Our collars didn't get turned. Dad sewed our buttons on. The collars wore out through scrubbing the dirt off using a scrubbing brush and Sunlight soap on a scrubbing board. There were no washing machines for ordinary folk in those days.

The bag-wash

There was what was called "The bag-wash". It wasn't very good for the clothes as buttons got ripped off and things got torn. You took your washing to the bag-wash shop in a sack with a number on it which the shop had provided. You left your washing there. You would collect it the next day still soaking wet. Everything came back tangled up and it took ages to untangle the different items and even longer to iron them. After a while the clothes started to tear because they were washed in such strong chemicals. I believe they were washed in the bag. That's why it was called the bag-wash. The sheets came back from the bag-wash smelling lovely and clean, scented with bleach.

We only had what was called a "flat iron" in those days. It was made completely from iron. It was very heavy and it got very hot, even the handle. It was heated on the gas ring. You had to hold the handle with a cloth when you were ready to use it. The clothes often got scorched because the iron would get too hot. When our iron was not in use it held the back door open.

My Uncle George mended my shoes. He was so kind to me. I used to beg him, while he was mending his own family's shoes, would he please mend mine, because, if my dad mended mine, I would probably never walk again.

My dad always left nails sticking up when he mended my shoes. They used to cripple me. I was always having to put cardboard in my shoes for two reasons: one because of the holes, two because of the nails.

Nowadays people would think you were very poor if you had holes in your shoes or you had to put cardboard in them to keep your feet dry. But that was normal in those days - everyone did it, because families were much bigger and poorer.

In those days families passed their clothes on to each other when they didn't fit any more. It was nothing to be ashamed of. (Bill wouldn't wear mine.) My cousin Kathy and I swapped clothes a lot. We always looked as though we had a lot of things. We used to pretend we were "well off". Mum and Dad were both bringing money into the home now but there was nothing much you could buy with it if you didn't have the coupons.

We were better off than a lot of families as there were only Bill and I. We were considered to be only a "small family". That upset me because I hated being part of a "small" family. I wanted lots of brothers and sisters. I thought my mum was mean not having lots of kids. After all she'd had lots of brothers and sisters.

My aunties always came to our house to talk to my mum when they needed some advice. But, like all families, everyone would join in with their two-pennyworth. We kids would "ear-wig" and giggle, especially when they were discussing something private.

Our house was always full of my mum's brothers and sisters - Anne, Lizzy, Kitty. Then there was Elsie - she was a sister-in-law. She was married to my mum's brother, John. Mum had three brothers - John, Alf and Reg. She also had two brothers-in-law, George and Bob. My mum's name was Ellen, usually called Nellie. Nana's name was Kate and my Granddad's name was Jack.

Auntie Anne was married to Bob Wood. (I had been Auntie Anne's bridesmaid.) They had two children, Catherine and Charley but Catherine died at three years old. She caught diphtheria. We were all very sad and cried for a long time. Later the twins, Janet and Margaret, were born. Auntie Liz was married to George Ward. They had three children - George, Joyce and Sylvia. John and Elsie had six children. John, Kathy, Valerie, Vivien, Rita and Jesse. My mum, Nellie, was married to Harry Wright and had two children me (Rosie) and Bill. Auntie Kit, my youngest auntie, was courting Fred Walker. They got married later and had two children, Katherine and Bill. Alf and Reg were as yet still unmarried.

My mum had asked Dad if he would give Auntie Kit away. I didn't understand this expression at the time and I felt very sorry for my Auntie Kit, having to be "given away." My dad had this honour because he was our only male relation still in England at this time and he was able to get compassionate leave. All the brothers at this time were in foreign lands. But, for now, my aunties were either living with us, or their mum, because their husbands were away fighting and it was best to stay all together if at all possible. My aunties would come around to our house to get ready for a night out. My nana was a bit religious and wouldn't agree to the married ones going out dancing. She would moan at them and tell them off if they put on too much make-up. Our kitchen always smelt of "Evening in Paris" perfume, which you bought in Woolworths. We kids called it "Evening in the Alley" or "Evening in Billingsgate".

My mum would help my aunties get ready for a night out. Mum was a dab hand at doing their hair. She would heat the curling tongs in the fire for an on-the-spot "pageboy", an angelic style used for little angelic pageboys at weddings; or a "bang" which was a sausage-shaped fringe. I can still remember the smell of burning hair when the tongs had been left in the fire for too long. But, at the end of these beauty sessions, if all had gone horribly wrong, out would come the "snood" (a long black crochet hair-net) or the "turban" (a triangular scarf tied around the head). It was really for hair protection in the factories but the women adapted it for leisure-wear by stuffing lots of newspaper inside it and making it stand out. I liked these two styles and intended to wear them myself when I got older, but times change and they went out of fashion.

Nana didn't like my aunties going dancing, even though they all went to the dance hall together. Girls went out in groups of about twenty in those days and they would all stay together in the dance hall. They also danced with each other most of the night as there wasn't much male company about then. When the dance hall closed at twelve o'clock they would all come home together, arms linked and singing *Show Me the Way to Go Home* or something like that. But, despite the war, going out was just a bit of fun for my aunties while they still could. They were not very old and who knew what was around the corner? I must say it did seem strange not seeing many young men about. But things did change later, when our boys came home on leave and the GIs and the Allied soldiers arrived; POWs too (prisoners of war) but that's another story.

Ordinary people sang a lot in those days. It is what people did. No-one took any notice. People would sing as they walked to work or went shopping. The men always whistled tunes. We always knew when my dad was home as he would whistle coming down the street - *All the Nice Girls Love a Sailor* or T*he Fleet's in Port Again*. I could never understand why he did this as he was assigned to essential war work for the airforce. My dad was stationed nearby so he got home quite a lot.

People went to the pictures a lot during the war. It helped to forget the misery of the times and what was going on outside. There were dozens of cinemas, all showing lovely films that would make you laugh or cry but never make you blush or give you too many nightmares. I *lived* in the cinemas. I went to them all - from Finsbury Park to the Holloway Road, Highbury Corner to the Angel. Kings Cross to the West End. All these cinemas had their own characteristics. They all had their own noises, like the sound of the tube trains running beneath the cinema; there were all kinds of weird rattles and rumbles. The Regent Electric Picture House in King's Cross had the lot. As you watched the film, you could hear the crash, bangs, wallops, rattles, whistles, even the hissing of the steam trains in the King's Cross mainline station.

You could also smell the steam from the massive train engines. You could hear the porters yelling at each other to be heard over the noise of the trains. The Regent Picture Palace was only a stone's throw from the King's Cross goods yard and mainline station. We didn't mind all this racket; we hardly heard it, we were lost in our film.

At the beginning of the war the government closed all picture houses and dance halls and cancelled all sport and entertainment. After a few months they realised what a mistake this was since these things helped boost the morale of the people; thus they reopened them all again.

On the move again

Mum was thinking that it was time to move on again, for the umpteenth time, this time away from Finsbury Park. We were forever on the move. We had moved many times from 1939 to 1941-42, always in the Finsbury Park area. But Bill and I were both growing older now and needed a bedroom of our own. Sometimes we had to move rather quickly before the rent-man or the tally-man called. We would have to do a "moonlight skip" because Mum could not pay the bills.

It wasn't as if we were poor; Mum simply had better things to do with the money. If it was a genuine move we would leave a note on the door to let people know where we had moved to. Dad said he never knew where to find us when he came home but he always did. He would find us through one of the family.

It was easy to find somewhere to live in those days. All the houses were in a bad condition owing to the bombing and the bomb blasts which made most of the houses unsafe, almost condemned. Some should have been. Landlords were only too glad to let people pay rent to live in them.

Most of these houses were bug-ridden and it took days of scrubbing with Lysol, Ibcol and carbolic acid to try to get rid of them. Mum also put down mountains of DDT. It took ages to get rid of the little blighters for they were under the wallpaper. We used to watch them crawl out of it at night, then Mum would hit them with her shoe. When Mum hit them it made me feel sick because they used to "splatter" - that was because they were full of blood from biting someone. They were bloodsuckers. (I have always had a queasy stomach, not surprisingly.) We also sprayed the bugs with liquid DDT. They survived but it nearly killed us.

These bugs had a good breeding ground because most people decorated their walls with wallpaper and when it was time to redecorate they just put the new paper over the old. Most people used a flour and water mixture as wallpaper paste. In a couple of the houses we moved into the paper was six layers thick! The reason the paper was kept up and papered over so many times was because the layers kept the wall together. It was the done thing.

Another of the houses we had moved into was 86 Isledon Road. It was just down the road from the famous Astoria Picture House with its beautiful entrance hall. It was just off Seven Sisters Road, Finsbury Park.

This house was such a wreck that the ceiling fell in on us during our first night there. We had to sit on the stairs for our safety until it was light and we would be able to get help.

After that little incident we stayed with our nana for a time. Nan was now living at 416 Liverpool Road, Highbury, Islington. Nana had rented two rooms at the top of the house and, as you can imagine, it was very cramped. By then my aunties were also living independently. Anne had moved into her own place - she had rented two rooms in the house next door to Nana - 418 Liverpool Road. Mum went house-hunting again. It was quite exciting as you never knew where you would land up.

Mum was unhappy in the Finsbury Park area as she really wanted to move back to Islington. Mum, even though she originally came from Clerkenwell, only felt at home in Islington. We were always moving - we could not settle anywhere - and Bill and I were finally getting a little fed up with it. Since the war had started we had moved so many times we hardly had a school long enough to call our own - or a house for that matter. If any of my uncles were home when we moved house it would be fun as they let Bill and I ride on the barrow with the furniture.

Another of the houses we lived in was right by the side of our new school, Stroud Green Junior Mixed. Our house was 56 Woodstock Road. That was near the back entrance of Finsbury Park which we got into by crossing over the railway bridge. Through this entrance you could turn right to the tennis courts, football pitches and swings. If you turned left you came to the boating lake, cafe and the band stand.

Finsbury Park was fenced off from the main Seven Sisters Road. It had its own roads inside the park. These roads from Harringey to the Manor House and Seven Sisters Road were full of the army's war machines. There were weapons like anti-aircraft guns and searchlights. Most of the big guns were on the backs of lorries. This was so they could be moved at a moment's notice. There were Bren gun carriers, Bofois guns and the ack-ack guns; I believe the ack-acks ran up and down on the railway lines. There were also landing craft; we called them Ducks. They were amphibian vessels like those used in the Normandy landings.

There was also barrage balloons. These were gigantic silver balloons (they looked like big floating marrows) which went up miles into the sky on wires. These were to trap low flying German bombers and the fighter planes which sometimes escorted the bombers.

Clissold Park had the same equipment. Every park had these weapons - searchlights, barrage balloons and guns. Some of the searchlights were also fixed onto the backs of lorries. These weapons of war were our toys when they were not in action and we would play on them. No-one seemed to mind very much, and the soldiers just chased us off. We would run away and come back later.

Bill and I could name all the guns as they were fired at the planes in an air-raid. ("It wasn't arf a racket!")

In this house, 56 Woodstock Road, our school wall was also our garden wall. Even then I was always late for school and I must admit I hated it. We had a basement flat in this house which led right out into the garden. This was the first time we had ever had a garden we could play in; it was lovely. Dad got carried away with this garden and went out and bought us a live chicken from Petticoat Lane so we could have fresh eggs for tea. Dad would sing, "Hey little hen, when, when, when, will you lay me an egg for my tea?" It turned out to be a very vocal cockerel so Dad decided to kill it for dinner. He tried to wring the poor skinny thing's neck; it made lots of noise, swearing, swarking and beating its wings which frightened us. Bill and I kept shouting, "Leave it alone, Dad," which he did in the end and the bird escaped, living to tell the tale.

We never ate it and we never got an egg from it. But that was not the bird's fault! We called it Cocky after its ordeal because it would strut around our garden with its head on one side either glaring at us or completely ignoring us, depending on what mood it was in. It could not hold its head up straight any more. I thought my dad was very wicked.

Lots of people kept chickens for eggs and for eating. They also kept rabbits for eating. But!! Families got used to their animals and made pets of them and wouldn't kill them.

In our garden there was an Anderson shelter. It was horrible. The shelter was half-filled with water and it stank of mould and sulphur. The old lady from the ground floor of the house slept in there. She was enormous. I don't know how she got in or if she ever came out as we only ever saw her in the shelter. It was quite a drop from the garden to the bunk bed which she slept on. I was always wondering how on earth she got down there and I never did find out as my

32

mum wouldn't let me ask her. Mum said I shouldn't be so rude.

The shelter was much too small but at times we had to stay in it if the raids were very bad. One night the raids started as usual. Mum, Bill and I were bundled into the shelter; my dad and Ernie Gibbs, the man who lived at the top of the house, stayed on watch outside the shelter, all keyed up about an impending German invasion.

At about midnight they both heard a creaking noise, the sort of noise a descending parachute would make. Ernie and Dad hid and when they saw it was a parachute landing in our garden they both jumped on it. "It's all right, Ernie," Dad said; "I've got the bastard," to which Ernie replied, "I've got him as well, Harry." They both gave this German a hefty blow only to discover they were fighting each other. There was no German! The parachute had been carrying a mine and that had fallen out of the basket over the school. Thank God it never exploded.

This incident caused a laugh in the family and Dad never lived it down with my mum's brothers. They always greeted him with, "Hello Harry, caught any Germans lately?" or, "It's all right, Ernie, I've got him." Dad never had much of a sense of humour. But I thought he was brave. Mum wanted to move out of this house because she had seen an unexploded bomb go straight down one of the manholes in the school grounds and no-one would believe her. So the hunt was on again. Everyone was looking for a place for us now - Nana, aunties, uncles, friends...

Our house

Our uncle, Tommy Wiley, came up trumps. He had seen this empty house in Islington. His wife, Ena, had then got in touch with my mum.

Mum soon found the owner, who was a Mrs Rogers and within a few days we moved in. Mrs Rogers had moved across the road to be with her daughter. She told Mum the house was haunted. Bill and I never saw any ghost. Mum said she had and told us it was a little old lady. Mum called the ghost "Gran". I think Mum was just playing a trick on us to make us frightened and to make us behave ourselves if we were playing up.

We all fell in love with this house the minute we set our eyes upon it. There were no ifs or buts - we wanted it. This was the first time we had all agreed on the choice of the house. We were now going to be living in Islington. We were going to live near our nana and aunties. For once things seemed to be going all right. Bill and I had been fed up for a long time, either living in places we didn't like, or with people we didn't like, or who didn't like us. (Can you believe that?) This was to be the last time we would move. We had a whole house to ourselves.

51 Rhodes Street, off Mackenzie Road, Holloway, London N7

This house was a funny kind of house because it had no back rooms. We had six rooms, all front facing. Only the stairs were at the back of the house with one window which looked out into our backyard and Adam Place, a little cul-de-sac where there was a paper factory and a closed down sausage factory. In our backyard was the lavatory, an air-raid shelter and the wash-house. This wash-house had a coal water heating boiler which boiled the water for you to do your washing. It also had a mangle to wring the water out of the clothes before you hung them on the line. The water supply in the wash-house also supplied the house. We had to bring the water into the house by the bucket-full.

Our yard was about the size of a postage stamp. The back door led out into Adam Place, St George's Road, and Eden Grove. (Our new school was in St George's Road - it was called St James's.) This road had a pub and a church almost next door to one other. The church was called the Sacred Heart. The pub was the Victory, Vic for short. On Sundays, we kids would watch some of the "saints" or "sinners" come straight out of church into the pub. It used to make us laugh. Secretly I envied them. I always thought I would like to be like them. These people always seemed to be happy, not like my teetotaller family.

Their kids would be allowed to sit in the pub doorway and have lemonade and arrowroot biscuits. (These biscuits were the size of a plate.) I was green with envy. I was one of those kids who always thought the grass was greener in the other field. I longed to be happy like them. I wanted to really have a good laugh. I wanted to drink beer, smoke fags and sing; I thought I was missing out on life. I was nine and a bit years old.

In the midst of all this feeling sorry for myself, Mum, Liz, Kit, Elsie and Anne started to work on the house. They cleaned the house from top to bottom, ripping the old wallpaper from off the walls and just painting them with distemper. Every room was a different colour.

Dad came home for a few days and plumbed the water into the house from the wash-house, although we still had to go outside to the loo. What luxury! Bill and I had a bedroom each. Mum and Dad had a bedroom of their own too. We now had three bedrooms, a kitchen-come sitting-room with two empty "damp" basements plus running water. We weren't to know then just how many times we were going to have to share our house, our basements and our bedrooms with our bombed out family and their pets or that this house would nearly be the end of us as well. But what you don't know can't hurt you.

I didn't mind our family coming to our house. I loved it when my aunties, uncles, cousins, Nana, Uncle Tom Cobbleigh and all were there because I felt safe. Hitler couldn't hurt us if we were all together. They were good company for our mum when our dad was away. They were always cheerful and made us laugh. At times we kids slept in one big bed, head to toe like sardines and we would have a good giggle. It was fun.

We made lots of friends in our street and the surrounding area. There were lots of families. We had marvellous games and we got up to a lot of mischief. There were the Shaws, Riders, Fishers, Limbys, Staffords, Coopers, Burgesses, Wards and Wrights. We played knocking dolly out of bed, Tin-can Tommy, cricket and rounders, hits and spans with our marbles, and flicks with our picture cards. We swapped our comics and made our own scooters. We pinched milk bottles off door steps and sold them to the recycling depot for a penny each. We collected and sold jam-jars to "Manzes", the pie and mash shop. We tied string across the pavements and tripped the drunks up as they came out of the pub, arm in arm, singing *Show Me the Way To Go Home*. They would all trip over the string and fall in a heap to the ground, cursing and swearing,

!!*!*!*!*, waving their arms and legs, and thrashing about on the pavement. We all thought it was very funny.

Rhodes Street was a very long street with air-raid shelters built all down one side: it was separated into two unequal parts by Lough Road cutting across it. Our part was known as Little Rhodes Street. Little Rhodes Street started with a grocery shop. The lady who owned the shop, Mrs Mac, lived on the premises. We were always knocking her up for something; she used to grumble but she always served us if she had what we wanted.

There weren't a lot of animals about at this time. The government had suggested that people had their pets put to sleep when the war started. This was in case an animal was left on its own if the owners got bombed out. The reasoning was that the pet might get hurt or starve if left to fend for itself. (What's worse than being dead?)

At this time of shortage in the animal kingdom the houses were being overrun by rats and mice. The rats and mice were attracted to the pig bins which were left in the street to collect waste food for the pigs to eat. The dustmen were paid extra money to collect the pig bins and take them to the cooking depots to be made into pigs' swill for the pigs. These bins were very smelly in the summer and infested with maggots and bluebottles.

We had more than our fair share of rats and vermin because of having the paper manufacturer and the sausage factory at the back of our house. There was also a paper collection depot at the front of our house, just down the road a bit at the junction where Rhodes Street joined Mackenzie Road.

To help us get rid of the mice and rats, Bill and I went out and pinched someone's cat and brought it home under my coat. There were no questions asked and the cat liked it with us and stayed. We also owned a dog who had followed me home and stayed. I named him *Rex* - like a king: this was written on our money - GEORGIUS VI D: G: BR: OMN: **REX** F : D: IND : IMP. Rex helped a lot with our rodent problem. The government had now changed its mind again and was asking for dogs to help get rid of the rats. They had decided it was not such a good idea after all to have had all the animals put down. While all this was sorting itself out the war was still going on around us.

V . . . —

Chapter Three - The Second Evacuation - 1940-1941

Air-raids were carrying on as usual. But things were beginning to hot up. Hitler was changing his tactics again and his plan was to bomb Britain into annihilation. Hitler wanted to break Britain's spirit. He wanted to destroy London utterly. Once again most of the children were to be sent out of London. This time, because we were expecting real trouble, Bill and I stayed with Mum.

We were expecting what was being called the Blitz on London. German bombers were soon flying overhead. Bombs were raining down on us. We were all now using the air-raid shelters. People were terribly frightened, the young children who were not evacuated cried themselves into an unconscious sleep in the shelters every night. It could not be called real sleep; it was pure exhaustion. We were worn out with the sound of the sirens, the droning of the bombers, the exploding of the bombs and the constant noise.

Older children tried to control their misery by hanging on to Mum. Sometimes babies cried and others just whimpered. Mothers had to be strong for their children but secretly they just wondered what this was all about. They wondered if their husbands, who were away, knew how they were suffering and what was happening to them, or whether they knew how near death or injury their wives and children might be.

Some of the neighbours would come into the shelter moaning, "Not another bloody air-raid," while others came in with their hair in curlers and dressed in their nighties carrying a thermos flask of tea or a little tipple of something, "for medicinal purposes of course." Some carried a paper carrier bag with their family photos and all their worldly possessions in it. The shelters were packed every night even though the comfort left a lot to be desired.

Because we all had to sleep in the shelters some ground rules had to be made. 1) No-one was to come in drunk. 2) All adults had to go outside the shelter to urinate. 3) No-one was to belch or fart as it was not very nice for the children. We kids would giggle when they did even though we didn't like them doing it. We would put our heads under our blankets to escape the smell. There were no windows in these shelters. When they were packed you felt you were being suffocated. There was a lot of weird smells like wintergreen ointment and sulphur ointment which the old ladies rubbed in their aches and pains.

We all tried to help each other keep our spirits up with jokes about the Germans, the "Fatherland", the "Master Race". Some of the people tried to sleep while others snored their heads off. Through all this was the constant noise of exploding bombs. When the all-clear sounded the weary people picked up their kids, their bits and pieces, and went back to their homes, that is if they still had one. At least we had survived another night.

By now the war was getting very nasty. Bombs were dropping willy-nilly all over the place. There were raids day and night. It was just savage destruction. People said that surely nothing could be worse than this. London refused to crumble and the people prepared. The Londoners sandbagged the doors, sandbagged the windows, sandbagged anything that could smash and cause injury. This was going to be a battle, a battle of the people, a battle of the Great City of London.

They prepared the shelters and opened the tube stations for deep shelters. Then it started! The Blitz - twenty-eight days of constant bombing from the 7th September 1940 to the 5th October 1940. Ton upon ton of bombs. We had no sleep, no food, no clean clothes and possibly no home when we could get out of the shelter to have a look.

The East End took the worst of it - Stepney, Poplar and Rotherhithe, all Docklands. 7000 people were killed, 9000 injured and thousands homeless. The German planes pounded London with wave after wave of bombs. The enemy planes flew low over the city following the Thames and bombing anything and everything they passed over. They bombed the Woolwich Arsenal, the power station and the gas works all in one night.

London took eleven hours of constant bombing on another night. The city was a sea of flames. Lots of people were sleeping down on the underground stations. They were using the tubes as deep shelters. People from Wapping to Mayfair, rich and poor alike, slept down the tube. On one Sunday morning in September 1940 people came out of their shelters to find nothing. Their houses were gone. Everything they knew or recognised was gone. They had nowhere to go. They just walked about aimlessly looking for friends, relatives and pets until the police, fire brigade or the ARP wardens picked them up and took them to rehabilitation centres. There the WVS looked after them and made them a cup of tea, then sent them to places where they could rest. London south-east had its blitz in the spring of 1941 when Buckingham Palace was hit. Big Ben was damaged but it still worked and the House Of Commons was damaged. 100,000 bombs were dropped from 500 planes in another all-night raid, and this was the heaviest yet. Thousands were killed.

We prayed for fog; we loved foggy days and nights. We loved our pea-souper fogs where you could hardly see a hand in front of your face. It made your cough and choke but we loved it, because on those nights there were no raids as the bombers couldn't see us. There was no radar at that time.

But when the nights were clear and bright with the moon shining, we were a sitting target. The bombers could follow the Thames. You can't hide water. And that's how there was such accurate bombing of the docks and the city. But our attackers were also sitting targets as our fighters could see them and they would go after them. We would watch the planes attacking each other. We would call them cat and dog fights. It was very dangerous to watch these fights as there was a lot of shrapnel flying about. We children would collect it after the raid was over.

One of the worst things I can remember is always feeling bits of grit in my hair from the falling debris all around us. I also remember being dirty. We couldn't even have a wash, sometimes for days. I hated seeing the sad face of my mum as she looked at Bill and me and tried to clean our faces with a piece of rag. She never cried but we sometimes thought she was going to cry, or she had been crying. When Mum looked like that it made us sad and it frightened us. Bill and I would say to her, "What's the matter, Mum? Don't look like that; don't look miserable."

When the German planes had passed over North London, going across to the East End and further into the city, we would come out of our shelter and have a look around. We could hear the bombs dropping on the docks and see the pillars of smoke rising and we knew what they were going through. It was a nightmarish time. The firemen fought a never-ending battle to put out the fires. London was an inferno. Most of the water mains in the docks area had been ruptured. At one time the EWS (emergency water supply) also ran out. Water had to be taken straight out of the Thames. At one time the Thames water dried up because the tide was low. It was mayhem.

Doctors and nurses worked day and night treating the injured and bombed-out people, somehow getting them to hospital if that was at all possible. If an ambulance couldn't get through the debris the police would get through with the help of the ARP and the local defence volunteers. These people would carry the injured out to one of the waiting police squad cars who would then take you to the nearest police station, where you would wait for an ambulance to pick you up and transport you to hospital.

The police stations were always crowded with casualties. Blood was everywhere in the police stations. Casualties were either laying down, sitting down or just standing. The police would bandage you up if you were bleeding badly or give you pads to hold to your wounds. They were very kind to the children, getting them to the hospitals in their squad cars if the ambulance was going to take too long to come. Things would still be blowing up. Explosions were going off all over the place. You didn't know if it was bombs or the gas mains - they all sounded the same to us kids. Through all this mayhem

the worn-out Londoners still held on. Hitler could not and would not crush our spirit. He might kill us. But he would never defeat us. Then, one day, after weeks and weeks of the Blitz and months of bombing, there was no air-raid warning over London. It just didn't come; it had stopped. We didn't know what to expect next. We didn't know what was worse - the waiting for something to happen or the certainty.

We didn't know what Hitler was up to. But we were soon to find out. Hitler had turned his evil attention on Coventry. Hitler blitzed Coventry with over 600 tons of bombs and thousands of incendiaries. The City was smashed to smithereens. There were so many people dead they had to be put in a common grave. Next they bombed cities and towns in the provinces; next places like Birmingham, Sheffield, Manchester and Glasgow.

They were trying to knock out British industry. After that they hit the ports with night after night of bombing. Some people were worried for their children who had been evacuated to the provinces.

"Goodnight Children, Everywhere"

Most people listened to the wireless in those days; it was the only home entertainment we had. It was run on a rechargeable electric cell, like a battery and it was called an "Accumulator". Bill and I, like all the children in England, listened to *Children's Hour*, which was on every evening from five o'clock to six o'clock. When it was finished Uncle Mac would say, "Goodnight children everywhere." Then they would sing a song to us London kids and to all the evacuated children and to children whose dads were overseas. They sang this song for any children who were separated from their families in any way or for any reason. It went like this:

> *"Goodnight children, everywhere, your mummies think of you tonight. Lay your head upon your pillow, don't be a kid or a weeping willow, just close your eyes and say a prayer, and if you have a kiss to spare. Even though you're far away, we're with you night and day. Goodnight children. Goodnight."*

We would then go to bed with our eyes prickling and stinging with unshed tears, tears that you never wanted anyone to see. The time would have been six o'clock in the evening. We would go to bed for a rest. We went to bed early so we could get some sleep before the air-raid warnings went, letting us know we were in for another night of no real sleep.

Once the German bombers came over there was no chance of sleep. Mum and Dad or Mum and one of her sisters would sit and play draughts or cards to pass the time away until the German bombers arrived. The siren would sound and we would be taken from our beds to the shelter. The raids were as regular as clockwork. You could set your watch by them.

Raids had now returned to London again but on a much reduced scale. We were told by the government that (only!!) 3,000 people a week were being killed in London. (Double it and you might get the truth.) We had heard Broadcasting House hit by a bomb while we were listening to Alvar Liddel reading the news and Buckingham Palace was bombed while the royal family was there. No-one was spared. Most of the men from eighteen years old to fifty years old had been called up long ago and were away on active service.

Most of the unmarried women were called up too. They were needed in the women's fighting forces: the WRNS (navy) and the WAFF, later the WRAF (air-force) and the ATS (army) and the Women's Land Army. "Dad's Army" or the Local Defence Volunteers had now come into being. This was made up of any man who could not go into active service; any man from seventeen to sixty-five years of age could join as it was voluntary. It was only men who could join, although the women were not far away to back them up.

Some of these brave men fought in the First World War but were too old to fight in this, the Second, World War. It was very comforting knowing that these experienced men were watching out for any sign of enemy invasion. It was nice to know they were there to protect us and warn us of any movement by the German troops who were hoping to invade British shores. It was really a "Dad's Army" with its Captain Mannerings and Sergeant Wilsons, Corporal Jones' and Private Pikes and Frazers, all full of patriotism and innocence and hopelessly equipped (as seen on TV today). These men didn't have many weapons to defend us with but they knew where everything could be found at a moment's notice. Everything was listed. They knew where they could get picks, shovels, hammers, spades. They knew who lived in the houses and how fit and willing they were to fight.

Everyone had a part to play. One job was to take all the signposts down to confuse the enemy should they reach our shores. I'm sure it would have done, as it confused us and we lived here. The Germans had reached the undefended Channel Islands. It was very eerie. The "Home Guard" came into being in 1941. I believe these men were armed. My dad became a Home Guard at some stage during the war as by then he was suffering from perforated ear drums.

Our nerves were being pushed to the limit. We were expecting the German invasion at any time. But even so, each family was ready and waiting for them with more than a little surprise!!! We had a "Shillelagh" (an Irish cudgel) We called it our "thumping stick". We were also expecting a poisonous gas or chemical attach. We never went anywhere without our gas-masks or Identity cards. We never strayed far from our homes so that our mums could find us at a moment's notice. We also didn't seem to know too much about what was going on. The newspapers were not allowed to publish details of where bombs had actually dropped or what damage they had done. Maintaining morale was paramount. The fewer disasters that were made known the better. It was also to stop the information getting into German hands. The newspapers didn't give us much news.

They only told you the good news about how well our fighting forces were doing or how many planes we had shot down and how many ships and submarines we had sunk. We never really knew what was going on. We thought that our planes never got shot down and our ships never sank. Even our forces were not allowed to tell you where they were or where they were going. It was all very hush-hush.

Most of the information on London we did get was by word of mouth and through the evidence of our own eyes. If there had been a bad raid where any of our family lived, when the all-clear went, we would get on our bikes and go down there to see if they were okay. I was always rushing around looking to see if my friends and family were all right. I was always very concerned for them. I hated the thought of them being hurt.

44

At times I couldn't bear it. Sometimes I thought I would just die from the sheer misery of it all.

As the war dragged on and bombs had dropped all around our area it seemed impossible that we had never been hit. We had our windows shattered a few times with the blast from exploding bombs but we soon got them mended and the glass put back in.

Dad would say, "Oh well, that one didn't have our name on it." If we stayed in the house when there was a raid on, Bill, Rex and I would get under the big dinner table for protection. We went under the table in case the ceiling fell in.

Bill and I would listened to the shrapnel hitting the metal dustbin in the backyard. When the raid was over we would go outside and pick it up. Sometimes it was still hot. One day when I went out in the yard to pick up the latest lot, one big piece had my initials stamped on it. RW. "Dad, Dad, look! It's go my name on it. What shall I do?" Dad just laughed and said, "You're all right now, Rosie girl, it missed you." I thought I was protected after that. Time passed. We dragged ourselves through each day, not knowing what would happen. It is surprising we had such a normal life. It can't be explained - things like doing everyday tasks, women having babies, children going to school, people making plans. It's funny the things that stay in your mind, like telephones. Looking back it seems strange how things worked. In those days there was no telephone communication between ordinary people. There were public telephones (I don't know who used them) in which you put four pennies and pressed button A for an answer, or button B to get your money back. But there was no-one you could phone.

No-one we knew had a phone. It was fun going round pressing the button B to see if anyone had forgotten to get the money back. It didn't happen very often but when it did there was great excitement. We all had a gob-stopper. (a great big sweet that changed colour when you sucked it - it was the size of an egg). If there was too many of us we all had to share and take a turn at sucking the gob-stopper. We even took turns with the chewing gum. We were not fussy. My mum used to go mad and say that I was filthy. Bill never did anything like this. Bill was too fussy.

We now come to 1944, the last year of the war. We had been hearing a lot about Hitler's Secret Weapon. It was called the V I - it was a pilot-less plane. The Londoners called it the "buzz bomb" or the "doodle bug"; you were safe with this plane until the orange light went out and the engine stopped. Then you ducked into the nearest shelter for safety. There was no accuracy with these weapons. These V Is killed approximately 6,000 people and injured 18,000. Eventually our code-breakers, with the aid of aerial photos, found the factory deep in the heart of Eastern Germany and bombed it. That was the end of the V I; but not the end of the nightmare. There was worse to come. Just as we though it was all over, the V2 came along. The V2 was Hitler's ultimate weapon.

The V2 was a long range rocket; travelling faster than sound, carrying a ton of high explosives in its war-head, it came without warning. When it was near all you heard was a tearing sound, just like an express train. If it was too close you never even heard the bang. You were already dead. These were Hitler's ultimate weapons. He had thrown everything he had at us and failed. But one rocket did have my name on it.

On the 26th of December 1944 (Boxing Day) we got bombed out by a V2 rocket. Mum, Bill and I were listening to ITMA (*It's That Man Again*) with Tommy Handly; it was a comedy programme on the BBC. It was about 10.30 p.m. The rocket came without warning. We were not expecting anything because it was still the Christmas holiday. The rocket scored a direct hit on the Albion pub in Mackenzie Road - where my friends were sitting in the pub doorway eating their arrowroot biscuits and drinking their lemonade and waiting for their parents who were inside still celebrating Christmas. They were killed. Many of the people we knew were killed in that pub on that Boxing Night. Entire families perished - mums, dads and children. It was classed as one of Islington's worst tragedies. The same rocket that fell on the pub knocked our house down too.

All I can remember is a bright flash, a whroosh, then my dog, Rex, and I were thrown across the room. We both landed on the sofa; then everything came in on top of us. I must have lost consciousness for a while as the next thing I can remember is struggling to get up and finding bricks and glass and the windows on top of me. I was covered with something wet. It turned out to be blood. I knew it was because I could taste it. I did not know at this time that I was quite badly injured.

My left eye had something in it and it hurt. My hair was stuck to my face with the blood and dirt. I called Mum and Bill but they didn't answer and I couldn't see them. I called Rex but he didn't come.

I made my way to where the door should have been and called for help because there were no stairs and I couldn't get down from the top floor. The stairs and the front of the house had gone. They had been blown away in the blast. While I was calling and struggling to get out of what was left of the house in case it caught fire a light was flashed in my face and a voice said, "I've got a casualty here. I think it's a little girl." I looked round to see who it was. I was the only one there.

They asked me if there was anyone else in the house. I said that my "mum and brother" were and I asked the ARP man if he could get them. I never mentioned Rex; I already knew the dog was dead as he didn't get up when I did and he didn't follow me when I called him. I did not cry, there didn't seem much point. I was taken to Caledonian Road Police Station by the ARP wardens, then onto the Royal Northern Hospital in Upper Holloway, where I was admitted as an orphan. They found out much later that Mum and Bill had been got out of the house uninjured and I had been left for dead. I was to be rescued later. My dad found me in the Royal Northern about six weeks later. I said it was about time. Dad said everyone had been searching for me. I was taken home to the hostel that Mum and Bill had been moved into at Highbury Barn, right next to Avenell Road and the Arsenal football ground.

The accommodation at the hostel was one bedroom and a shared kitchen which I didn't like because some people had dirty habits. This made my nerves bad and made me feel sick. I started to suffer from blackouts. So it was decided I should go and live with my nana in Liverpool Road near Highbury Corner. While I was living with my nana her house was blasted by a V2 rocket that dropped on Highbury Corner.

I was once again thrown across the room. I caught the blast right in my face again! My head had swollen up like a pumpkin and my eyes were just slits.

Mum and Bill realised that Highbury had been hit by the rocket and quickly came to see if we were okay. When Mum saw my face she fainted. Great, I thought! What about me? My mum was getting all the attention. I was taken back to the Royal Northern Hospital. The doctor said I was all right but that I should rest. He wanted to send me away to the country but I said no, I wouldn't go. I wanted to stay with my family. No-one argued. I stayed. A few days after that incident I became very unwell. I had to visit our own doctor who examined me and diagnosed me with **German Measles**. I could not believe it - it was a joke in the family for quite a long time.

I was nearly twelve years old now. I had been bomb dodging since I was six. I was hoping this war would soon be over as Hitler was getting too near to me. I can't remember how many more rockets, bombs, incendiaries and other things Hitler hurled at us. It didn't seem to matter. For some reason I just didn't care anymore. After this last lot I felt sure I was going to die. I wasn't even scared - just resigned. Tears didn't come easily any more. We were all mentally worn out with the bombing night after night.

All our emotions seemed to be paralysed. We had become almost brutalised. I mourned my friends when they were buried with hardly a tear, just utter disbelief that I would never play with them again, never knock the dollies out of bed anymore with then or trip the drunks up; never see them eating their arrowroot biscuit or drinking their lemonade on the pub doorstep. I was too shocked to cry.

Children played a big part in this most horrible war. We were put through the most mind-numbing misery and deep soul-destroying heartbreak. We witnessed the death of our friends, our families, our pets. We had seen them lying hurt, bleeding and dying. We had been dug out, injured, from our own homes after an explosion, dirty and covered in debris. We were a sacrificed generation.

After the war the king sent a message to every schoolchild in Britain. But before we got that letter we were going to earn it. And earn it we did. We suffered air-raid shelters, air-raids, bombing, injury, death, evacuation, separation, rationing and sheer misery. We watched the cat and dog fights with the German and British fighter planes and saw the Battle of Britain with our own eyes. We saw the spitfires knock the German planes out of our skies.

As we watched, mesmerised, shrapnel fell around us. Air-raid wardens threw us to the ground and laid on top of us to shield us from the bits of flying metal. We lived through the Blitz on London which nearly wiped us all out. We saw it destroy our homes, our schools, our churches and kill our friends, families, and pets.

We had to have ugly, frightening gas masks to protect us from poison gas. We had V1 flying bombs and V2 rocket bombs dropped on us with no warning. We also had incendiary bombs and anti-personnel bombs dropped on us in air-raids. Our shores were littered with land-mines because we were expecting German invasion any time. We stood dumbfounded as we witnessed the first atomic bomb dropped on the people of Japan and saw the devastation and suffering it caused then and still does now, more than fifty years later.

We witnessed the end of the war, first with the victory in Europe, then with the victory in Japan. We celebrated the victory and the end of the war. But only with the dropping of the first atomic bomb on Hiroshima, on the 6th of August 1945 and the second atomic bomb, dropped on Nagasaki, on the 9th of August 1945, did the war come to a complete end.

My generation has never been completely free from fear and doubt. We have never been able to feel completely safe. There have always been wars and rumours of wars; it has never stopped. There was the Suez Canal crisis in the fifties that nearly caused another war, the Iron Curtain and the "Cold War" with the USSR. We never knew which way that would go. Then there is always the Middle East bubbling away with one crisis or another.

Let us hope that the world leaders can deal with all these problems and realise there is nothing else to fight about. In reality all the dragons are slain. Let's put our energies in fighting pollution and hunger, anything to help our planet.

The King's message to the children of England

Today as we celebrate victory, I send this personal message to you and all other boys and girls at school. For you have shared in the hardships and dangers of a total war and you have shared no less in the triumph of the Allied nations. I know you will always feel proud to belong to a country which was capable of such supreme effort; proud, too, of parents and elder brothers and sisters who by their courage, endurance and enterprise brought victory. May these qualities be yours as you grow up and join in the common effort to establish among the nations of the world unity and peace.

V . . . ▬

V . . . —

Chapter Four - We Make Haste Slowly

Peace had been creeping slowly upon us for a while now. We had began to hear of the terrible things that had been happening to the Allied POWs in the concentration camps in Germany - things we had no idea of as the POWs in England seemed to be treated all right. We started to hear the names of places that films are made about today, names like Auschwitz, Belsen, Colditz, Dachau and Ravensbruck (a women's and children's concentration camp).

We went to the News Theatre to watch the Allied soldiers liberate the Belsen concentration camp. We watched horrified at what we saw. We watched as the starved, sick prisoners tried to welcome the liberators who had come to get them out of this concentration camp. They were just like walking skeletons. Some, could hardly stand at all. Others were so ill and weak, they just lay on the floor; they didn't even have the strength to stand up. They had been starved for so long; they were just living on a handful of rice a day. There was nothing left of them, they were just skin and bone. Their eyes were sunken and lifeless. Their teeth protruded from their lips because their skin was stretched so tight. Their legs and arms were like match-sticks. There were dead bodies lying on the ground where people had died and had just been left to rot. Disease was rampant.

Some of the prisoners were dressed in the striped pyjamas suits which were the camp's uniform for the prisoners; others

bove left: Uncle George goes to war
bove right: poster in Watford Museum
Below: baby in the much-hated gas mask

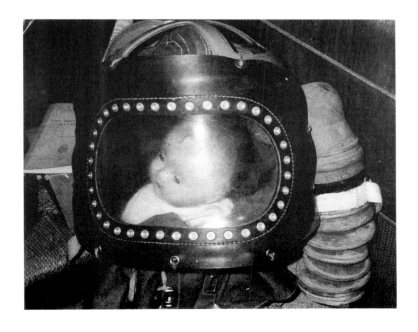

Top: typical sight in World
War II - gas mask alongside
various articles in the
kitchen
Above: the author's
grandmother - Nanny Bailey
Right: John Bailey joins the
navy post-war, and helps to
keep the peace

Above: a typical Andersen shelter

Above left: the ill-fated Rex with
Nanny Bailey
Top right: the young Rose
visiting Nanny, Auntie Ann &
young cousins
Bottom right: Rose's mother
back from war-time shopping

Top: Not an unusual sight - bomb damage to a shop
Above: Typical street party to celebrate the end of war
Below left: Auntie Liz dressed up to the nines. Below right: young
love - Auntie Anne & Uncle Bob

were naked except for a piece of rag tied around them like a nappy.

When the Allied soldiers entered the Belsen camp, the first thing they did was to give the prisoners some food. Some ate the food immediately and died. The food they had been denied for so long proved to be the final blow. Their poor worn-out bodies were beyond eating. They could not digest the food. They would have to be on a diet of bread and milk for a long time to come. As we sat watching these captured soldiers we were thinking these men could be our dads, brothers, husbands, sons and uncles. The people in the news theatres just broke down and cried. This story was to be repeated time and time again as more of these concentration camps were liberated. These camps also had women and children in them but it made no difference who you were to the SS.

As more and more countries and concentration camps were being liberated by the allied forces, and all the atrocities were coming to light, and Hitler had most definitely lost the war, Hitler shot himself. The "Fuhrer" was dead, so was Eva Braun, his wife, who had taken poison. Goebbels poisoned his six children, shot his wife and killed himself. They were all dead. Some people said, "good job"; others felt cheated. What a mix-up everything was. You didn't know what would happen next. It was one thing after another.

The news pictures also showed us the liberated people in France, Poland and all the other towns and cities, walking aimlessly about, not really knowing what to do or where to go. At first there was no order to things but, as the allied troops settled in, things got more organised. For the time being, though, many different peoples were on the move - Jewish people who had survived the concentration camps, the gas chambers and the death marches; Civilians who had been deported from their own occupied countries to be used as forced labour in Germany and the German occupied countries; allied Prisoners of war - all the flotsam and jetsam of the war's human victims, all trying to get back home. Home, please God, to families, peace and sanity, which was hardly likely, as all of Europe was in tatters. They just wanted to be able to put this terrible war behind them.

They never wanted to hear again the "Heil Hitler" and the clicking of the heels, no more to see the Swastika arm bands, jack boots, the Nazi salute. For these people and the people of Europe, the war was over.

V . . . ▬

Outside in the streets of London it was mayhem. Even though we had not yet had the official notice from the King and Churchill that the war was over, victory was in the air. Shops brought out red, white and blue bunting and Union Jack flags - anything we could wave and decorate our windows with. My dad had made a gigantic wooden **V . . . ▬** which was the Morse coded message that told us the war was over in Europe

By May 8th people could wait no longer; they just started to gather down the Mall to Buckingham Palace to await the news of Germany's surrender. We wanted the news from the King himself. At six o'clock in the evening, on May the 8th, King George VI broadcast to the nation. It was something we had all been waiting for - proper confirmation from our King that the war was over.

Part of the King's speech

> *"Much hard work awaits us in restoring our own country after the ravages of war. And helping restore peace and sanity to a shattered world."*

People had gathered from far and wide to listen to this speech. Buckingham Palace was floodlit.

The King and Queen came out on the balcony waving Union Jacks. The people went crazy. Then the King, Queen, Churchill and the two princesses, Elizabeth and Margaret, came out on the balcony. Princess Elizabeth wore a WRAC uniform. Princess Margaret was still a schoolgirl

Later the Queen acknowledged the women of Britain, Thanking them for their magnificent war effort in the fire service, ambulance service, police service, the WVS and the civil defence. The Queen also said, "Maybe what we women have suffered in this war may indirectly save our children and our grandchildren from another." Churchill then gave a speech from the balcony.

54

Part of Churchill's speech

"My dear friends, this is your hour. This is not a victory of a party or of any class, it's a victory of the great British nation as a whole. We were the first, in this ancient island, to draw the sword against tyranny. After a while we were left alone against the most tremendous military power that has been seen, left to face the might of the German forces alone - and prepared to fight.

We were left alone for a whole year. We stood alone. The lights went out, the bombs came down, but every man, woman and child in the country had no thought of quitting the struggle. London had to take it. So we came back from the jaws of death, out of the mouth of Hell while the world watched and waited. Let us brace ourselves to our duty and so bear ourselves that if the British Commonwealth and Empire lasts for a thousand years, men will still say THIS WAS THEIR FINEST HOUR.

Churchill also thanked the men and women who worked round the clock, in the Home Guard, in the fields to produce food, in the factories to produce munitions, in offices, shops, schools, hospitals. He thanked the young barely trained RAF Spitfire pilots who took to the skies to defend our shores with the battle of Britain. The crowd was in a frenzy, singing *Land Of Hope And Glory, Rule Britannia,* and *For He's A Jolly Good Fellow,* followed by cheers and hurrahs at timely intervals.

V . . . ⎯⎯ *It's over*

Suddenly it was all over; Britain took to the streets to celebrate victory in Europe. All you could hear, wherever you went, were jubilant people saying, "It's over, it's over." The real knees-ups were in Piccadilly. Piccadilly Circus was packed solid. Everyone was kissing each other. "The war is over." "It's over, it's over." We just kept on saying it.

That night there were lots of American Service men at the Dilly, and allied service men - lots of soldiers, sailors, airmen, also lots of girls, girls, girls! I was in the West End that night; I was where all this action was going on. I was with my brother Bill. All I could say was, "Got any gum chum?" to the Yanks, and touch the sailors' Dickies. (Ha-ha, that was the name for their collars!) I was twelve years old. All through my life it has always been the same - I have either been too young or too old for whatever was going on.

Although the war was over in Europe, it was not yet over in Japan. Australia didn't celebrate VE day with us as they still had men fighting the Japanese in Borneo. By the time the Japanese surrendered, Australia had lost more than 40,000 soldiers, sailors and airmen. Our soldiers, about 1,000 of them, were fighting alongside the Australians in the Borneo rain forest. Australian POWs had been moved from Singapore to Sandakan in Sabah in the spring of 1945 to be used as slave labour to build an airfield. These Australian POWs had been ill-treated and were starving, naked, and ill, but they still had to toil for their handful of rice. When the airfield that they were building was finished the Australian soldiers were marched inland, in batches and they were shot.

A memorial garden was built in view of the summit towers of Kinabalu in Kandasang in remembrance of these men. Mount Kinabalu is the highest mountain in South East Asia, 7,500ft.

All this suffering finally ended when Japan surrendered after two atomic bombs had been dropped on them in the August of 1945: VJ Day - Victory in Japan, VE Day - Victory in Europe. The war in Europe had already been declared over. It was all coming to an end.

In reality there was no single day on which the Second World War ended. A line had to be drawn somewhere. One day had to be agreed upon, so it was May 8th that was chosen as Victory in Europe Day - and the end of the war for us. But individual wars still went on for sometime.

V . . . —

Chapter Five - Knowel Hill School

1945: the war is over. For a few months everything was going just fine. There was still a lot of excitement in the air and lots of things were happening. Children were being brought back home from their evacuation and the service-men were being demobbed from the forces. There was a lot of coming and going and loads of confusion. Once again people were left to their own devices. The ammunition factories were closing down now and the women who had worked in them were now being put out of work. The soldiers, sailors and airmen who were coming home to "A Land fit for Heroes" also found there was no work for them to do either. So history was repeating itself as once again there were no jobs. Food and clothes were still in very short supply and there was no money coming in. This caused arguments and fights between the husbands and wives, and the children suffered.

These men, past heroes, were just aimlessly wandering about looking for work. These men needed help. They were traumatised from what they had seen and experienced during the war, but so were we from what we had experienced at home. We were in no condition to comfort them and they were in no condition to comfort us.

Family life had changed forever. Some families were still grieving for their dead relations and for their destroyed homes.

The very young children, "The War Babies", the ones who had been born during the war, didn't even know who their fathers were. This "coming home" from the war was the first time they had met them and their lives until then had been without a father figure. They didn't know what to make of their fathers when they finally appeared. Who is that man kissing mummy? Who is this man staying in our house? This situation was the same all over the country - all over the world I suspect. So the "coming home" of our dads turned out to be the most miserable time and that which we had so looked forward to was now a nightmare. Our dads had changed. They were not the happy-go-lucky men that went away to fight against tyranny. But we were not the same either. I knew I had changed but I didn't quite know how. I felt so rebellious.

I would spend most of my days in the picture houses so that I could lose myself from my miserable existence. I spent many happy hours in the Savoy Cinema, Holloway Road watching *State Fair*. This film was a musical with Danna Andrews in it. I was in love with him and James Mason, Frank Sinatra, Bing Crosby, Johnny Weismuller, (Tarzan of the Apes) Allan Ladd, even Abbot and Costello. The list went on and on.

I loved them all. I would stay in the cinema all day. The programme would start at about ten-thirty in the morning and run continually till eleven o'clock at night. I stayed in the cinema all day from ten till six, and then I had to go home. It was quite a let-down to have to come out into the bomb ruined Holloway Road after all the lovely places I had been to all day at the pictures. There were a lot of musicals in those days. I loved the *Ziegfield Follies* and the MGM girls and their lovely dancing. One of my favourite films was the *Dolly Sisters* - they were Betty Grable (The Legs) and Jane Russell (The Bust). In my mind's eye I looked just like them. (I didn't though.) Both of them must have been six foot tall; I was only five foot high and I had legs like a footballer and a bust like a sparrow; I wasn't even beautiful or sophisticated.

I looked so young that if there was a "A" classified film on I had to get someone to take me in as you had to be with an adult if it was an "A" film. It was so embarrassing. My friends could get themselves in. I could only get myself in when the film was classified a "U". So the best thing to do was to bunk in. I nearly always bunked in anyway as I never had any money and Mum didn't have the ninepence to give me - well not just for the pictures. I would wait at the back door of the cinema for someone to come out. When they lifted the fire escape bar on the back door I would sneak in.

I would quickly make my way to the ladies toilets which were in the same passageway as the fire escape and the back entrance, then I would enter the cinema through the ladies toilets. It was easy.

Most of the cinemas were all built in the same style and it was easy to bunk in. When a lot of us went together only one paid. They then let the others in through the back door. It was a bit more difficult if there were boys and girls as we all had to come out of the same toilet, so sometimes we got caught and thrown out. It was all a big giggle. We were so young in some things and so grown up in others, although you are not a child if you have lived through a war.

At this time I was still suffering from the effects of the head injury I had received on Boxing Day 1944. Even though it had been a good few months ago I was still having what the hospital called "blackouts" (becoming unconscious and not remembering it afterwards). I was finding it hard to sleep. I couldn't stand the silence. I would lie in bed, night after night and my ears would hiss because it was so quiet. I would have to cough just to hear a noise. Sometimes the trolley bus antennas would slip off the overhead wires as they criss-crossed at the Nags Head and Hollow Road and make a flash. I would duck under the bedclothes, with my eyes tightly closed and wait for the bang, which, needless to say, never came. It was the same with the trams. If you had the wireless on and couldn't hear what was going on outside, the tram wheels rolling on the tramlines would sound like the tail-end of the air-raid warning. We called it "The moaning mini". I was always listening out for trouble. I would always be saying, "Shush, what was that?" or "Did you hear that?"

I was becoming a nervous wreck. It was not like this while the war was on. I knew where I was then. I knew what to expect and what to do but now in peace time I could not cope; I couldn't bear not being able to sleep and never relaxing, just waiting - for what? I lost all purpose in life. It was such an anti-climax, this peace. What had the war been all about? I couldn't see that anything was different. It was just as before as far as I was concerned. I couldn't concentrate because I was exhausted. This got me into a lot of trouble everywhere.

At school I was forever getting into mischief and getting told off. I hated school. The more I got told off, the more defiant I became and the less work I did. I was becoming a wild child. Eventually they expelled me from school.

I never went back even though the education authorities and school governors said I must! Instead I went to work helping on the stalls in the markets, or minding people's cars for them while they went shopping. I liked doing that. I used to pretend they were mine and let any of my friends who might be passing by sit in the cars with me for awhile. I did all sorts of odd jobs to earn some money - walking people's dogs, taking their babies out in the pram while they got on with their housework, chopping wood, getting their buckets of coal in from the coal-hole for them to have ready for their fire in the evening when everyone would be home; collecting wooden boxes from the market and chopping them up into sticks, then making up the sticks into bundles and selling them round the doors for twopence a bundle. I couldn't sell enough of these bundles of wood; everyone wanted them. I also would pinch the wooden tar blocks from the roadworks and sell them to the housewives for sixpence a pram load.

I was enjoying doing all these things but the authorities hadn't finished with me yet. I landed up in court. I was said to be beyond parental control. I was sent away to an approved school for a maximum of three years. It was my own fault that I was sentenced. I only had to say I would go back to school, say that I was sorry and that I would turn over a new leaf. But I didn't. Instead I said I wouldn't. I gave the judge some cheek.

I told him he couldn't "make" me go back to school and, who did he think he was? Hitler?" - not quite the right thing to say so soon after the war. The school was in Kenilworth, Warwickshire, I was about thirteen years old.

I was determined to be as naughty as I could. I played hell in this place, at first fighting everyone. I spent many months in and out of solitary confinement where a team of social workers, doctors and psychiatrists would come to visit me. I told them to leave me alone and to buzz off - well, that and a few other horrible things which I cannot bring myself to put in print now.

But they in their wisdom decided I had been affected by the war. I was quite indignant. I told them I thought it must be them that had been affected, not me. I said I thought it was they who needed sorting out. How could the war still be affecting me if it was over now? Their system of treatment was that the more I was naughty, the better they treated me. I just could not understand it. I flew into crying tempers and lashed out at anyone who tried to comfort me. I would not let anyone touch me.

I hated them. I only wanted to be home with my mum and brother. Eventually I started to listen to them. I didn't have much choice. I found it was better to just sit there listening than to keep fighting. I was worn out. They had began to wear me down. I was made to realise I was not bad but that I was a sad, frightened and lonely young girl. In response to this soft and kind approach I started to tell them all my worries - worries about my mum and my brother Bill, about the anxiety of not knowing for sure that when you all said goodbye in the morning as you left for school, or Mum for work, whether we would ever see each other again; how the stomach would churn when the air-raid warning sounded. Where did that bomb drop? Was Mum okay?

I spoke about the noise of the bombs whistling down and the explosions, about night raids and feeling vulnerable and helpless in the blackout, about going to sleep through exhaustion and still waking up exhausted; how I had lost friends, our house and our belongings with the bombing. How I had been injured and separated from my family for two months believing I might have been orphaned. I told them about my dog getting killed and all the other terrible things that had happened and all the sad sights I had seen. I told them about missing my extended family when they were evacuated, about not having enough coupons for things, about there not being enough food for my mum to eat properly as she gave most of it to Bill and me. I also told them how I worried about my nan, my aunties and cousins, how my family were my whole world. I told them about the dirt in my hair, about not being able to wash.

I talked about bugs, fleas, ringworm, scabies and impetigo. I was so angry.

These talks went on for months. It was all coming out now. They couldn't stop me. I just went on and on. I was mad, mad about being bombed out at Christmas, mad that my friends died. I was mad that my dog died. What was the war to do with him? I was mad for all the sad little dirty snotty-nosed orphaned children. I was mad for all the dead children and their sad families. I was mad that London was all smashed up.

Most of all I was mad with Hitler. I wanted to kill Hitler myself for causing all this upheaval and unhappiness. But he managed to duck out of any revenge we could have on him, by killing himself, by committing suicide.

While I was at Knowel Hill School, they were very good to me even though I was disobedient and wild. I felt like a caged bird - trapped. I made one last attempt to prove I was tough. I ran away. I was soon caught. It was easy for them to catch me as I had never been in the countryside before, at least not for any length of time. I had never had to run across big fields with animals in them. I only knew the streets, alleys and ruins, where I could duck and dive and hide. They would not have caught me if I had run away in London.

Anyway that's what I told them. I felt silly being taken back after only a few hours' freedom. They told me they were expecting me to abscond. I couldn't understand. Did they read minds? After my detention in solitary confinement, which only lasted a week, I was allowed to mix with the other girls again.

My running away was never mentioned any more and I was beginning to wonder if I had ever done it. The staff at KHS (Knowel Hill School) liked me for some reason; I didn't know why but their kindness was grinding me down. I started to like them. I didn't want to like anyone; it was too painful - I would have to worry about them. What if they went away or died? But I did like Mrs Jewel, our Deputy Head Mistress and Mrs Spriggs our Head Mistress.

Mrs Jewel had a little dog and she let me look after it. That little dog helped me to settle down. I told the dog all my troubles, all the things that bothered me. I told him about the war and Rex my own dog and all the troubles I had seen. I would cry into his fur and he would lick my tears from my face.

I started to behave myself. I did my school work; I even learnt to sew and knit. I was surprised at myself; I was even enjoying the things I was doing.

Girls were coming and going all the time, as part of this school's work was to assess where you went to from there. Some of the girls went home. Others who had no homes joined the airforce. The school was run through a military arrangement. Mrs Spriggs had been watching me and had decided it was time to put my case up before the board to see if I was ready for home leave.

I got turned down because I was cheeky at the interview. I was cheeky because I didn't like the way these people in authority spoke to me. I did not like being spoken down to in such a condescending manner. I just wanted to be spoken to and treated like a grown-up, not like a small delinquent child.

Mrs Jewel and Mrs Spriggs were very disappointed with me. I said I was sorry. I promised that I would do better next time. I also remembered that it would be another six months before I could be put forward again for home leave.

Mum and Bill came to visit me. They had bought me a watch for my fourteenth birthday. Mum looked lovely. She was wearing a new dress. I was very proud of her. Bill was the same as ever, he never looked tidy. His socks were down in his shoes and his cap was all skew-wig.

I looked at his coat sleeve. Thank goodness he did not have the snail trail which would have been down his right sleeve. He was now wiping his nose with a handkerchief. Billy was growing up. He just kept looking at me and saying, in a kind of grown-up voice, "When are you coming home, Rosie?" I said I didn't know and I thought of the home leave I had just thrown away and I wondered if he knew about it but I didn't say anything.

I was allowed to show Mum and Bill around the school and the grounds without an escort; I felt very privileged and trusted. We had tea in the little reception room and after that it was time for Mum and Bill to get the train to go home. I waved them goodbye at the school gate. I didn't cry because I knew it would upset Mum and Bill. When their taxi was out of sight I went back into the school and straight to my dormitory and cried. I was very sad and lonely. The poor dog got another load of misery told to it. I started to feel better and I made a conscious effort to be good so I should be able to go home again.

I was beginning to grow up. I was still wearing white socks and bottle green knickers and a fleecy lined Liberty Bodice. I thought it was high time I got back out into the world and did something for myself and help my mum.

For some reason I never went back in front of the Governors again but I was granted home leave. I went home for two weeks. I was surprised how small our house was after living in KHS. I hated the lavatory being outside in the yard, I hated the "Po" under the bed and the slop bucket in the kitchen under the sink. I hated myself: I was turning into a snob, the very kind of person I hated the most.

By the time I had been home for a couple of days and had visited my nan, aunties and friends I realised they all still had "Pos" and slop buckets so I didn't mind any more.

Then it was time to go back to KHS. I nearly hated it again, but I decided to grit my teeth and go back and stick it out. It was only a few weeks after my home leave that I was granted, right out of the blue, a trial release.

I was so surprised; I never knew this was being arranged for me. I went home on a month's trial. I never had to go back again as my release was granted while I was still at home. I never really went back to school either. I had to stay home while the authorities tried to fit me in somewhere. But time was slipping by, as by then I was nearly old enough to start work.

My brother Bill was still at school. I was always glad when it was time for him to come home as I was bored all by myself. I would go to meet Bill from school. We would then both go to school teas.

We had to go to a different school for our tea as Bill's school, St James, didn't have any dining facilities. We went to a school called Ring Cross, which had a large dining hall and catered for most of the schools in the area. Ring Cross supplied both dinners and teas.

For tea we had a slice of bread and jam, a piece of currant cake and a cup of tea. It was lovely. I ate mine all up. Bill was fussy and wouldn't eat, so I ate his as well. He didn't like school teas but I did. I wanted to go to school dinners as well but I was not allowed to as you had to belong to a school which would order your dinner for you, whereas you could just drop in for a school tea.

V . . . ▬

Chapter Six - A Good Day's Work

I never had much education as a result of the war, although I must admit it was my own fault as I used the air-raids as an excuse to stay away from school, saying I was "too tired" through being up all night. Most of the other children still went to school. When an air-raid warning sounded in school time, we could either go home or stay in the school and sit under our desks for shelter, or sit in the school corridors away from any windows. St James was only a little school and only had two classrooms. It had been a "Doll Factory" in a previous existence. It got rather cramped in the tiny corridors when both the classes were in them and it was dark and suffocating. I always chose to go home, dragging my poor brother Billy with me because I was looking after him.

When the all-clear sounded I would not go back to school. I would go and bunk into the pictures for a few hours. Bill didn't like doing this - he was frightened. Bill was a good boy.

I was very proud of my brother as he was quite clever. He had taken after my dad and was a natural mathematician. He passed his Eleven Plus with flying colours and went on to a good school and a good career later.

I was wasting my time reading comics while Bill was at school. When it was time for our mum to come home from work, Bill and I would go to meet her. Mum had now found herself a little job in Ronalds Road in an ornament factory called Kingslaws. It was near where we lived, at Drayton Park, just about five minutes' walk down the Mackenzie Road.

The time had passed by very quickly since the war had ended. I was now old enough to go to work; but what was I going to do for a living? I could not do the odd jobs I did before because I was grown-up now.

I did ask my mum if she could get me a job with her in Kingslaws factory. She didn't seem to like the idea very much. She just went very pale and said "not so blooming likely". I seem to have had that same reaction from everyone in my family when I asked them to let me work with them. I gave up asking.

The hunt was on; I found that for every job that I applied for in writing, I was turned down flat. I didn't even get an interview. But, if I just turned up and asked the boss for a job, I always got it. I sailed through interviews with no problems. My dad said I had been blessed with the gift of the gab.

I skipped from job to job. I didn't like any of them. They were all nothing jobs. They ranged from making Christmas Crackers to toothpaste tubes, from making jewellery to spraying clocks or making radios on a printed circuit. I was an apprentice window dresser in James Selby's, a shop assistant in Jones Brothers and I worked on a stall in Chapel Street next to Alpino's cafe, where all the boys learning "the knowledge" met (i.e. budding taxi drivers).

I could not settle in any of these low paid jobs. I wanted to be my own boss, so, at fifteen, I decided to go it alone. But where should I start? I put my thinking head on and looked around. I went to markets, I looked in shops, I spoke to people and picked their brains. I knew there was something I could do but what was it? First, I needed to get some money! How was I going to do that? I looked around my house for inspiration and for anything I could sell, anything that my mum didn't need. I also asked all my family if they had anything they didn't want.

My nan and aunties collected some bits and pieces for me from their friends and I started to get quite a large collection. Everyone thought it was a big joke but I stuck to my idea. I opened up our two empty basement rooms as a second-hand shop.

These rooms led out into our backyard where there was a back door which led out into Adams Place and St Georges oad. People could come around to the back door so as not to disturb anyone in the house. It was perfect.

My dad had got a job at St Dunston's, making furniture parts for the blind ex-service men to put together and sell. However he was on night work and needed to sleep during the day so we had to keep quiet. I asked all my friends and neighbours to come to my sale and I asked them to tell all of their friends and neighbours.

The day I opened the basement shop I was amazed. I sold everything I had. With the money I made I bought more stuff and so it went on for a few months, but soon my dad was moaning about the noise. People were not going around to the back door but were knocking on the front door which was making Prince bark (another little stray dog I had "found"), which in turn woke my dad up. It was like "Casey's Court" Dad said - I was making a blooming "Poppy Show" of the house.

Mum said she was embarrassed when people knocked on the street door looking for "junk". She told them to go around to the back door and that it was nothing to do with her. I felt a bit put out about all this and thought it wouldn't harm Mum if she gave me a little bit of encouragement. I pressed on.

I bought and sold anything and everything, from crockery and cutlery to ornaments, clothes, furniture - anything people needed to put their homes together again. I even sold my own bed. My dad went mad when he found out. He went into a frenzy. He jumped up and down with rage. I had never seen my dad go so wild; "I will never ever buy you another bed," he yelled, and he didn't.

By now the game was over. I knew once my dad found out what I was doing he would stop me. I knew he wouldn't like it, and after the bed incident I thought it best not to argue.

I closed my shop and sold all my bits and pieces to the Rag and Bone man and the second-hand shop in Holloway Road. It was a shame because the business was going like wild fire. It had been a great success. But I knew I would have to move on soon as the business was getting too big for our basements. People were buying everything; they were even turning up with barrows to take the things away.

I experimented and had many new adventures with business - some good, some not so good. I always had money and I always enjoyed what I was doing.

Our house had been rebuilt after the rocket had blown the front off. It had got a new roof and a whole new front. I was upset. I was hoping they wouldn't repair it and we would get one of those nice new prefabs that were being erected on all the cleared bomb sites. These prefabs had inside toilets and "real" bathrooms. They were for the people whose homes could not be repaired and for the homeless people whose husbands were being demobbed from the forces. The land that the Albion pub had stood on was never re-built upon.

Mum and Dad never mixed with our neighbours anymore. They didn't mix with anyone. They "kept themselves to themselves". Every one called them Mr and Mrs Wright, a bit miserable I thought as my mum wasn't really like that; she was fun. She always seemed different when Dad was in. Dad was a very serious man. If you laughed too much he would say, "Laugh all day, cry before nightfall."

Dad was a gambler - he loved the dog tracks and horse tracks. Bill and I would go with him to some of the race meetings. When we went to Ascot or the Derby he would give us a pile of programmes to sell. We could keep the money for food and ice-cream. We would have to go and find him at the end of the day so we could get the train home together. Some times he had won wads of money, other times he was skint, but he always looked contented enough.

I spent my youth at the dogs - Haringey, White City and Walthamstow, etc and I liked it. I enjoyed the excitement. Dad never made his gambling pay. He had worked out a good system for winning but he could never stick to it.

We never got on very well. He didn't like me very much because he said I was wild and he never knew what I would do next. He said that I must have really been the milkman's daughter as I didn't take after him or anyone else in the family. I hoped he was joking - the milkman was a miserable old so and so, worse than him.

I did manage to throw the spanner in the works a few more times. In 1949 I met, and later married, an Italian boy and had five beautiful daughters in as many years. I got divorced and married an Irish man and got divorced again.

It was only to be expected said Dad, "knowing your track record!" Bill married Jose but didn't move out of Rhodes Street, continuing to live with Mum and Dad for a few years.

They had a daughter, Jane. Then they got a divorce. Both remarried. Bill married Pam and they went to live in Kent.

We were never really to move out of 51 Rhodes Street, only by marriage and eventually my dear Mum's death. The house was finally demolished and Dad was given a newly built flat in the Caledonian Road opposite Pentonville Prison. He loved it and stayed there for a few years, then got very ill and had to give up the flat to come and live with me in South Oxhey near Watford, where I had moved in 1968. Dad stayed with me for two years and then he too died.

Bill and I did get on in the world, despite the war and, in my case, in spite of myself. I did became a business woman; my husband and I opened a factory and we employed twenty full-time staff. We made "Ornaments" and I had two stalls on the high pavement in the Holloway Road selling ornaments and religious artefacts and one stall in Highgate, selling ornaments and crockery. We also "done" the fairs. Later, with my husband John Girolami, we started a car breaking business in Holloway N7, then later another at the bottom of Chapel Street, yet another on the Docks in Pennington Street, E1 (now called Tobacco Docks). More recently I have had a stall in Watford Market and South Oxhey Market.

Now at the grand old age of sixty-four I have gone back to college. I am studying at Cassio College for a Word Power III Certificate and A level English. I have already been at the college for two years, one year on a Return To Learn scheme and one year on an EAL - Essential Adult Learning course. I have four City and Guilds certificates in Word Power and three RSAs in Clait IT. I have passed a spelling test. I am very proud of myself. I only wish I had done all this when I was young. I am doing a GCSE in English in September 1998.

So life still goes on. Whoever would have thought that this would have all come about when the bombs were falling down on us and we were afraid for our very lives. So I close this story but it is not the end.

Now that I am old and (not!) ready to go
I start thinking what happened a long time ago.
I had a lot of kids, trouble and pain,
But yes, I would do it all again.

From *Kisses Sweeter Than Wine*

V . . . —

V . . . —

Chapter Seven - Another Memory Of War

by John Arthur Bailey

Born 18.10.31

Not long after the war started, all the park railings and gates were taken down for the war effort. All the railings and gates were also taken from houses and other non-essential premises. The fencing that used to divide our house in Highbury Quadrant from the tennis courts at the back was taken down by the council men to make ammunition for our fighting forces. All unneeded pots and pans were also collected for the same reason.

Because the tennis courts were not being used any more we would go onto the courts to play football, cricket, rounders and other games, and we were chased off by a policeman many times, though he did not bother us much as we were out of sight from the roads. But I think that some of the neighbours - the ones whose houses backed onto the tennis courts used to complain, moaning about children playing in the open spaces.

Over the years, and through lack of use, the courts had become overgrown with weeds. The border gardens had now become very overgrown and neglected. The man that attended the courts and gardens lived in our house.

But soon after the war started he and his family moved out, and we moved from the top of the house into his first floor flat which was just above the basement where Mrs "W" lived.

I was going to Gillespie Road School before the war - it was just off the Blackstock Road. It was a big Victorian type of school. My sister Elsie also went there. For us children from the "Quadrant" it was quite a walk. All I remember about this school is that I had to learn to write - "real writing"; I can't say that I like it very much.

During the war this school was closed down. I cannot remember exactly what happened but a plane that was shot down crashed into it, but the damage was minor I believe. At another time a parachutist got caught up in the structure after bailing out of his crashing plane. I was told that the Home Guard and police were involved in taking the German airman away.

A few doors away from our house was number 5 Highbury Quadrant, I made friends with the girl who lived there she was about eighteen years old, her name was Doris Skeret (or at least I think that is how it was spelt). She was courting at the time. She got married later and I had to call her Mrs Trievnor. Her husband was a Daily Mirror photographer; he was called up and served in the Royal Air Force.

During 1939 the threat of World War II was upon us. When it was finally declared most of us children in London and other targeted towns and villages were evacuated. Elsie and I went to a gamekeeper's cottage near Hitchin in Hertfordshire. They were very strict people, and I can say that we didn't like them very much. We had a long way to walk to and from school, and many a time we took a short cut by walking through the fields and woods.

Sometimes I was taken out on rabbit and pheasant shoots. Elsie would not go - she thought it was too wicked. I got told off for letting the rabbits loose when they were caught in the traps, it was legal to use these traps in those days. It was so cruel - a rabbit would be caught in two iron jaws and seriously injured; it could be left like that for days until someone came and put it out of its agony. We London kids could not understand such cruelty to animals.

This gamekeeper had big dogs that had to be kept in cages; he also had ferrets. The water we used came from a well. It was a very isolated place, but we made our own fun. We were not there for very long. Our parents wanted Elsie and me back home as there was not much happening regarding the war in England. No bombs had been dropped and people thought that the war would soon be over. Needless to say they were wrong. The war really started and bombs began to fall on London. Once again children were sent out of London to places of safety.

We were once again evacuated this time to 1 Beards Farm, Fremmington, Devon, near Barnstaple. The people here were a lot nicer, they had a son of their own so I had someone to play with. Once again I cannot remember the name of the people. I believe one of the family names was Snail.

The man of the family was a fireman. He use to take me out to different places. One place was near a river; on the other side of this river there was an aerodrome where we would watch the fighters take off and land. One popular plane that could be seen and was well-known, was the Lysander.

Our mum was missing us, so once again we were brought home, only to face all the bombing and enemy action in London. The first thing that Elsie and I had to do was go back to school, but a lot of the schools had been closed down.

So we had to go to a church school called St John's; this school was in Conewood Street which was off Blackstock Road; at the bottom of this street was the Arsenal Football Ground. The Headmaster was Mr Jarvis. Although strict he was fair. Mr Jarvis was in the Home Guard; at a later date he was made a Captain. At the assembly when Captain Jarvis came in newly promoted, he was in uniform and we all clapped.

Every year we would celebrate Empire Day. This Empire was made up of many countries - Canada, India, Australia, New Zealand and the African States. Most of these countries are now independent, so I do not think that Empire Day is now celebrated. The other day that was celebrated at school was St George's Day - St George of England.

During the winter our school was very cold as we only had a coal fire in the classroom. It was called a "combustion stove". Seeing that fuel was on ration and hard to get, the school had to be very careful. First thing in the mornings our hands were so cold that we could not write, so we had to try to warm them up by the stove. It was also very cold at the back of the classroom near the windows. In those days we had to keep our coats on. But like all schools in those days it was very hot in the summer because only the top part of the windows would open and we would all sweat cobs.

My sister Jessie went to a nursery near the school. I had to take her and bring her home as Mum and Dad were both working at a radio firm called Cossor; Mum was in the office while Dad was working on experimental work, trying to perfect the cathode ray tube for radar. At this time it was top secret, so he was not allowed to say anything about what he did, having signed the Official Secrets Act. When asked what he did, he would say that he was a storeman.

1940-42: It was at about this period that life began to get interesting. I was becoming more aware of what was happening. All my uncles had been called up, with the exception of Uncle Harry - being a cabinet maker he was put on essential work making aeroplanes - and Uncle Reg who was too young.

As I mentioned earlier, we had moved to the ground floor flat in the Quadrant when it had became vacant after the gardener moved out. This flat had very large rooms. They were originally two rooms with lovely marble fireplaces; they had been converted, one room into two rooms and another into three rooms. One of these rooms was still very long. It was in this room that Dad, Reg and Alf (when Alf was home on leave) would play cricket. Mum would be worried in case there was an accident. Her worries came true when the ball went straight through the window. Mum was upset, but as fate would have it, a bomb went off nearby, and blew the rest of the windows out, so it was taken as bomb damage and was repaired by the council. We still carried on playing cricket for years but used a ball made from paper. At one time when the Germans was dropping thousands of incendiary bombs on London, there were fires everywhere, the worst being in the East End and the Docklands. One of these bombs dropped

74

very close to our house and Alf jumped out of the window and put it out. Dad put one out that fell on the balcony. There was a lot of excitement.

Nan Bailey, Aunt Kit and Reg moved into the top flat that we had moved out of. This was during the early part of the war. They were not there for long. They moved to a street just off Drayton Park called Benwell Road. From this place they moved to Woodstock Road, Finsbury Park, near Aunt Nell. Uncle Harry, Rosie and Billy moved later to Liverpool Road, near Highbury.

Both Dad and Aunt Kitty were Air-raid Wardens (ARPs). At the back of the tennis courts a hut had been erected; it was the ARP HQ; an underground shelter had also been built for them. At one time my friend and I locked the wardens in this shelter. The opening was a hatch, so it could easily be fixed from the outside. Fortunately Dad and Aunt Kit were not in it, otherwise there would have been hell to pay. No-one ever found out who had locked the wardens in. Security became tighter after that.

The basement apartment had become empty when Mrs "W" moved out and it had now been let out to the RAF as there was a barrage balloon for them to look after on the tennis courts. However, this balloon was not there for long as the cable kept falling on the roof tops and doing a lot of damage.

There was also a barrage balloon in the Arsenal football grounds, but again not for long for the same reasons. It caused too much damage to the surrounding property. By now there were guns and barrage balloons in all the parks. Finsbury Park was very heavily armed. Mobile guns were in the streets. Light mobile anti-aircraft guns, pompoms and Bofor guns were common in the parks and streets. Clissold Park was at the bottom of the Quadrant and it had a barrage balloon, searchlights and guns.

Brick air-raid shelters and water reservoirs were built in the streets. Water reservoirs were built on bombed sights. Every day there were air-raid warnings; if we were at school we had to go to the schools shelter. This was no more than a school room that had been strengthened with iron rods and concrete, similar to the brick shelters that were in the roads. Sometimes we had to sit in the passage away from the windows.

We had to stay there until the all-clear sounded, which might not be for hours, or even the whole day. Parents could come to collect their children, and take them home and collect other children who might live in the same area, thus helping other mothers who had children at two different schools. If there was any real bombing we would have to go into the street shelters. At a later date, if there was no sign of any bombing in our area the headmaster would tell us to go home quickly. One of my main concerns was picking up my sister from the nursery.

I remember one time when a German plane came over very fast and low we could see all the details and the pilot. I think that the low flying was to avoid the radar. The pilot's purpose was to take photographs of the area, mainly of Cossor's.

Sometimes my dad would take me to visit his sisters. As there was a black-out the sky was full of stars, a sight that you cannot see today in the cities. When there was an air-raid, you could see the searchlights and shell burst in the sky; we had to be careful as the shrapnel would be falling from the sky and there were many injuries sustained by being in the path of these bits of metal. All the kids would collect shrapnel.

By now I had made many friends in our area - Roy Bishop, Gerald Pole and many more; we were all going to the same school. We would all go to Finsbury Park after school to watch the guns firing at the enemy planes if there was a raid on, only to get our behinds kicked and be chucked into the shelter, Being young we didn't realise the danger. When the enemy planes were not taking action against the guns, they were heading for their targets, mainly factories and airfields.

I was now finding my way around London. Dad used to take me to see my grandmother also his sister, my aunt Nell, who lived in Rhodes Street, Holloway. I would have great games with my cousin Rosie while her brother, Billy, was still a bit young and shy. I knew how to get to Aunt Nell's by myself, so I started to play truant from school to visit them and because of the air-raids I was not missed from school.

As I arrived at the house, Aunt Nell would be leaving for work and Uncle Harry was already at work, so Rosie and Billy would be staying in by themselves. Rosie would be looking after Bill. It must have been for weeks that I got away with this, but then, like all good things, it came to an end. I got caught. But this started a good friendship between Rosie and me which has lasted until this day. We were always seeing each other and shared the same friends. My sister Elsie was Rosie's particular friend. They went everywhere together. Elsie changed her name at this stage and called herself Kathy. There is only about eighteen months difference in out ages. Rosie loved Highbury Quadrant and stayed whenever she could. Rosie was afraid of nothing; she was always in trouble and she was always great fun. My mum thought a lot of Rosie. Aunt Nell and Mum were good friends.

During the war there was many shortages, one of them being coal. Many a time I would have to take the pram down to Drayton Park coal depot in Queensland Road. It was a long walk but it had to be done. Sometimes I would go all that way for nothing. But as Nan Bailey lived in a road nearby at that time (Benwell Road) I would pop in to see her and Reg, also Aunt Kitty if she was in, but most of the time she was at work.

As I said the coal situation would be bad at times so I would look for wood; some of this could easily be found at the bombed sites, although many a time I got chased off as it was dangerous. So I looked for somewhere closer to home and what could be better than the house next door? This had now become empty; the old lady who had lived there had gone away and like our house it was in dire need of repair. There were big cracks in the walls and parts of the ceiling were falling down, while the wall around the balcony was now in a very dangerous state. It was via the balcony that I got into the house next door. I started to pull the floorboards up for fire wood.

I had opened a lower window and left it unlocked so as to make an easier entry for the next visit. A bomb blew up some streets away and blew out the windows; it turned out to be a large land mine and the bomb squad got killed. Our windows got repaired but thank goodness next door's didn't but this left it open not only for us but also for other people to get in and take the wood. All the floorboards had now been taken, so I started to take the noggins out between the joists and then some of the joists themselves. The doors and window frames had been taken. It looked just as if a bomb had hit it.

The police had chased us many a time but I always made good my escape via the balcony.

Rosie and my friends were always playing in our old house. It was great fun; it was large and very spooky. There were also other empty houses close by but these houses were watched over by the neighbours, so we had to be more careful. But we had marvellous games; we would roar with laughter and scare the life out of each other. At times you could forget there was a war on.

Just up the road another house, No 13, had just become empty. This had been used by the Home Guard; it was their HQ. This house was watched a bit more closely, although we got into it sometimes, but we were limited as to what we could get out as people could see us easily. One incident did happen though; Aunt Edna, Aunt Bella and I went into the garden of No 13 to pick mulberries. I was up in the tree when a copper came in and caught my aunts red-handed as I was hiding up the tree. I was not spotted at first but, as luck would have it, the branch began to bend so I had to move up a bit, so the copper heard me and called me down. This copper was known to me as "Tubby". He asked my Aunt Edna what the idea was and she told him that as there was a shortage of fruit she was making some pies - it would be a shame for all that lovely fruit to go rotten. Tubby agreed and asked her to make an extra pie; he picked it up later, letting us off with a friendly warning and a nice full tummy.

I have had many a brushing with Tubby; he was always telling us off for playing cricket in the street, or "tin can copper", or knocking Dolly out of bed. Of course there was not many cars around those days, so playing in the streets was a common thing and a lot safer than it is today.

Barrage balloons couldn't be kept on the Arsenal grounds because their ropes kept catching on the stands and trees. The RAF had to clear this area. So the Arsenal caretaker let us use the grounds for our sports. I played cricket and rounders along with other boys and girls on this ground. We were allowed to use it because Finsbury Park had now become a storage place for tanks and guns, so making it a target area. That made it dangerous for us to go there for our games.

At about this time the Americans had come over, and were living in every possible place available. They moved into the basement flat of our house, after the RAF moved out. By now there were tanks and ducks (as they were called) and mobile guns everywhere and it was obvious they were to be used if there was an invasion.

It was about this time that Cossor was hit during a raid and a lot of bombs were dropping on our area. Because of all this activity we could not wander about as much as we would have liked to and we couldn't go into the house next door as often as we used to. Sometimes I would see a face looking out of one of the windows that had now been partly boarded up. I used to wonder who it might be, but I didn't give it too much attention.

One day, as I was coming home from school, I found the Quadrant crawling with police and the Home Guard. No 13 was roped off and we were stopped and told that there was a gas drill. I was not allowed to go through, I had my gas mask (which was always carried). I put it on and Tubby saw me home; I must have looked daft as no-one else was wearing one. Later my mother and father came home and the police began questioning them, the type of questions I didn't understand. Then Tubby turned to me and asked if I had seen any strangers in the area. First of all I said no, then I remembered the face in the window next door and told him. Then the police moved in, a man ran out, and went across the road to the church, jumping over the wall. But he realised he was surrounded and gave himself up. It was months later that I was told that he was a spy, and could have been homing in the bombers.

From the roof of this house you could see for miles. On a clear day you could see St Paul's Cathedral. This house was my favourite haunt; even though the lower section of the house was boarded up it still did not stop me, as I still had my old route in via the balcony.

During this period our family was friendly with the Skerets' and Mrs Treivnor who now had a son; sometimes I would go the play with him. He got rather attached to me, and would not eat his Sunday dinner unless I was there to feed him. His grandparents offered me money to teach him to ride a bicycle, since, like all children I was riding one. I was friends with the family right up until the time we moved to Dequincy Road, Tottenham and then we lost contact with them.

79

As the raids on London had now virtually stopped, people were beginning to return to London. So I was now making more friends - among these were Mickey, Rene, Hilda and her niece Hilary, also Shirley Roberts, Victor Davis, Jimmy Dazwell.

These friends were of the same age as me and we were always going out as a group. Rosie, Billy, Joyce and Reg would still be paying us visits, so were Ruth and Edna. We were still playing in the tennis courts even though they had now been completely ruined, but it made a good sports ground for us; we would play football, cricket, rounders and many other games. The only other people who were using a part of the court were the ARP Wardens (Air-raid Patrol). They had an underground office there that was bomb-proof. The wardens sometimes chased us off the courts, though it all depended on who was on duty. The wardens used to take a short cut by going through our gardens. We went across the courts to get to Sotheby Road, where some of my mates lived; the wardens tried to stop us but the residents said that they would stop them from going through our gardens if they did. There was just the odd awkward warden.

During the later part of the war, we were now being terrorised by the V1s known as buzz bombs, doodle bugs or flying bombs; in fact they were flying bombs. You would hear them and wait for the engine to stop; if it stopped overhead you would dive for cover. One did stop over our house but, as luck would have it, it glided over and dropped elsewhere.

The next weapon to be used against us was the V2 - this was the rocket. All you knew of this was a flash of light and a bang - you had no chance of taking cover. Auntie Nell's house was knocked down with one on Boxing Night and Rosie was injured and in hospital for sometime. Nan was also blasted out when one hit Highbury Corner.

The war was coming to an end and all hostilities against England had now stopped. This meant that normal activities were now beginning to return. I joined a club called the "Campaigners". We went camping in Surrey, not far from Bisley Rifle Range. It was used as a gunnery range by the army. There were plenty of bullets and other ammunition lying around; we were warned not to touch them but being kids we did. There was one incident that always stuck in my mind.

One day we went into the woods and found a mortar shell; a boy that we called "Buck" started to take it to bits and found himself left with a piece that had some hard substance in it so he started to dig it out with a knife. There was a flash and a bang and we all reeled backwards; then we all got up but noticed that Buck was still lying down. We shook him calling out, "Buck, Buck, are you all right?" but he did not answer. We started to get worried, and called out again when he suddenly got up and said, "Blimey! That was a loud bang!" and we all burst out laughing, still scared though. We left these mortars alone after that.

Another time we went for a walk into the village where there was a pond. We all went swimming in it. Someone told us to clear off. As we had to get back to camp early we left like good little boys. On our way back we ran into a road block and there were fire engines everywhere. We realised that the woods we had to go through were on fire. We were not allowed to go through. Some time passed, then the heavens opened up; boy, did it rain! The rain helped to quench the fire. We were allowed to continue on our way back to our camp. We were soaked to the skin and freezing cold. When we got back to the camp, we all made a dash for the cattle dip and jumped in (it was full of lovely clean water). The camp leader didn't know whether to laugh, cry or tell us off. The reason we had to get back early was that it was our turn to cook the supper; when he found out why we were delayed he let us off.

During our stay at camp we found some flat gadgets - they were round and made of metal. We started to take them home but, as they got a bit heavy, we threw them out of the train window. When we arrived in London the police and army were there; they started to ask us questions, looked through some of our gear and found one of these metal things on a boy. We were all quizzed, and told that they were very dangerous; they were practice anti-tank mines and while they would not harm the tanks they could kill people. We got scared and so confessed to the army bloke that we had thrown some of these things out of the train window. They then had the long, hard job of searching the lines for them. We just got a telling off and were sent on our way. We all gave a sigh of relief that we were not in any trouble and that we were still alive.

It was about late 1944 when I took up chemistry; a friend of mine showed me a place where I could buy all the equipment and chemicals - it was called Becks and was in Stoke Newington High Street. I got a book out of the library; it was about pyrotechnics, (fireworks). Yes, I was trying my hand at making some. To start with I made some explosive; I put it in a tin and took it to the best place I knew to try it out. That was in the air-raid shelter on the tennis courts. I managed to blow a part of the shelter up. The next minute as if by magic the sirens went. The wardens down the other end of the courts thought it was a bomb that had been dropped. Did we run? They never did find out what happened. Fortunately there was no damage to any of the surrounding properties. One of my friends who also made explosives had a part of his hand blown off. He made some very dangerous explosive and carried it in his pocket; due to the friction of walking it went off.

1945: this is the year that the war ended, first there was VE Day then VJ Day. There was jubilation everywhere - street parties, bonfires, fireworks the lot. But for me the most important thing was the fact that I left school in the summer.

At the end of war in Europe, VE Day, all the church bells rang - they had been silenced since the beginning of the war. The schools also rang their bells. The caretaker of our school rang ours for a few days, but because of other duties it was passed on to me, so I became the first pupil to ring a bell after the war. I was also head prefect. I was over thirteen and was looking forward to leaving at the age of fourteen to start work.

I started work at a small print shop called Cleveland Printing Works, Cleveland Road (I don't remember where exactly). I was to train as a compositor. The hours was 8 - 6 Monday - Friday and 8 -1 on Saturdays. The wages were thirty shillings a week (150 new pence) I used to get there by a 33 tram, then walk. I saved up to buy a bicycle. (This job set me up for the rest of my working life. I retired a few years ago, a fully qualified compositor with a daily newspaper.)

During this time all the brick air-raid shelters was being knocked down. The bricks were being crushed and being stored in the tennis courts. After some months it was like a huge mountain. At the same time people were dismantling their Anderson air-raid shelters which had been built in their gardens. This meant that they had to get rid of the corrugated sheets that they were made of. Some of these corrugated sheets were shaped like a j and some were flat. This gave me a brilliant idea. I used them to make a track down the mountain of broken bricks. I used one of the j type as a sledge, about six of us would get on at a time. The bushes at the bottom acted as a brake. We had a few accidents.

One day "Tubby" the copper came round; he saw what was going on and he asked me to show him how it worked. He came to the top of the mountain and just as I was about to get on he kicked the sledge away. Of course I was not on properly, and I caught my (NEW!) trousers on a sharp edge and tore them. Mum wasn't arf wild.

"Tubby" said it was dangerous and that he did not want to catch us doing it again; he never did but it didn't stop us. Some months later a lot more stuff was delivered and this practically sealed the tennis courts off. All the entrances were closed and that was the end of all our games on the tennis courts.

V . . . —

Bibliography & Sources

Awake and Watch Tower
The Rigway,
London, NW7 1RN

Islington Gazette
161 Tottenham Lane,
London N8 9BQ

Islington Public Library
Holloway London N7

Saga Magazine
Saga Building Middelburge Square,
Folkestone Kent CT20 1AZ

Watford Museum
Lower High Street
Watford
WD1